A GEOGRAPHY OF

# QUEENSLAND

Ian Wilson

CAMBRIDGE
UNIVERSITY PRESS

Published by the Press Syndicate of the University of Cambridge
The Pitt Building, Trumpington Street, Cambridge CB2 1RP, UK
40 West 20th Street, New York, NY 10011-4211, USA
10 Stamford Road, Oakleigh, Melbourne 3166, Australia

© Cambridge University Press 1994
First published 1994

Printed in Hong Kong by Colorcraft

*National Library of Australia cataloguing in publication data*
Wilson, Ian, 1925–
A geography of Queensland.
Includes index.
1. Human geography – Queensland – Juvenile literature. 2.
Queensland – Juvenile literature. 3. Queensland – Geography –
Juvenile literature. 4. Queensland – Geography – Problems,
exercises, etc. – Juvenile literature. I. Title.
919.43

*Library of Congress cataloguing in publication data*
Wilson, Ian, 1925–
A geography of Queensland / Ian Wilson.
    p.        cm.
Includes index.
Summary: Examines the various regions and environments of
Queensland, one of Australia's fastest growing states.
1. Queensland—Geography—Juvenile literature. [1. Queensland—
Geography.] I. Title.
DU260.W56 1993
919.43—dc20                                              93-17507
                                                                    CIP
                                                                    AC

*A catalogue record for this book is available from the British Library.*

ISBN 0 521 42714 2 Paperback

031040

## Notice to Teachers

Cover map: AUSLIG
Panoramic cover photography: Studio Sept

## Acknowledgements

Grateful acknowledgement is made to the following
(in addition to those acknowledged within the text)
for their assistance in both providing suitable material
and granting Cambridge University Press permission to
reproduce it in this text.

Australian Bureau of Statistics; Queensland Dept of
Lands; Queensland Dept of Environment and Heritage;
Queensland Dept of Primary Industries (Land
Conservation, Integrated Resources; Queensland
Forest Service); Queensland Dept of Resource
Industries; Queensland Dept of Housing and Local
Government; Bureau of Meteorology, Queensland
Regional Office; Water Resources Commission; Natural
Disasters Organisation; Brisbane City Council;
Maroochy Shire Council; The South Bank Corporation;
Queensland Sugar Corporation; CANEGROWERS; Moreton
Sugar Company Ltd; Queensland Newspapers Pty Ltd;
*Sunday Mail*, Brisbane; *Sydney Morning Herald*;
*Courier Mail*, Brisbane; UBD, Universal Press Pty Ltd;
Olive Piggott; Brian Williams; Danielle Koopman;
Frank Sanderson; John Wright; Greg Roberts; Tony
Koch; Gordon Collie; Beryl Lewis; Sonia Ulliana;
Bureau of Immigration Research, *Atlas of the
Australian People (Queensland)*, AGPS, Canberra
1990, Commonwealth of Australia copyright
reproduced by permission; *Review of Australia's Water
Resources*, 1985, Dept of Primary Industries and
Energy, Canberra 1987, Commonwealth of Australia
copyright reproduced by permission.

Every effort has been made to trace and
acknowledge copyright but in some cases this has not
been possible. Cambridge University Press would
welcome any information that would redress this
situation.

# CONTENTS

# PREFACE

Queensland, one of the fastest growing states in Australia, has an economy traditionally based on the natural resources related to the mining and agricultural sectors. However, in more recent years, tourism is becoming increasingly important.

This book examines the major features of the natural and built environments and the people of Queensland through a variety of student exercises and activities and a wide range of maps, diagrams and photographs. It may be used as the basis of a study of Queensland or for a comparison of Queensland with other states.

Because of Queensland's great biodiversity and the limits imposed by the size of the book, some topics/regions have been treated in more detail than others. Where specific detail is lacking, it may be an incentive for the students to do further research into that area which has aroused their interest.

Research topics have been included in each chapter. These research topics require the student to seek out and use resource material from libraries and other sources and so develop research skills and broaden their understanding of the topic. Students may work individually or in groups. If working in groups, each group could select specific sections and report back to the class after research has been completed.

When writing up the research topic make brief notes in your own words and avoid copying large sections from books. Also avoid cutting out, or photocopying, pictures and diagrams to paste in your report—use your own simple sketches, flow charts and other diagrams where possible.

Your teacher or librarian can assist by making sure that there are some suitable references available in the school or local library, so that you can make a satisfying start and be encouraged to seek further references from other sources.

The author has travelled extensively throughout Queensland and is currently a resident of the Sunshine Coast where he is actively involved as a tutor of geography with members of the University of the Third Age. His past experience has been in the field of geography teaching and curriculum development and in writing geography books for secondary school students.

# Chapter 1

# AN INTRODUCTION TO QUEENSLAND

Figure 1.1

Queensland is referred to as 'the sunshine state'. What images does this bring to your mind? For many Australians it is one of sunshine, golden beaches and sparkling blue waters! A place to visit on holiday—a respite from cold, southern, mid-winter days!

Does Figure 1.1 portray your perception (mental image) of Queensland?

1  What are your perceptions of Queensland? On a piece of paper make a list of the words which show your perceptions of Queensland. This activity can be done individually or with a group, when it is known as 'brainstorming'. Have you tried this type of activity before? If not, here is one approach. The class is divided into groups of about five people. One person in each group writes down words/concepts about Queensland as they are spoken by group members. The words are written down as they come to mind— no time is spent in discussion. There is no 'right' or 'wrong' word/concept at this stage. Allow about ten minutes for this. Now, rearrange groups so that each new group consists of one member from each of the other groups. Each person should have a copy of their original group's list.

Quickly check the various group lists against each other and add new words/ concepts that your group may not have included (remember—no discussion). Part of your list may be like this:

- beaches
- pineapples
- sunshine
- coral
- hot
- rainy
- cyclones
- Dreamworld
- holidays
- a big state
- Surfers

Hold a class discussion to decide on some headings. They could be the same as the chapters in this book or you may decide on your own set of headings. Return to your original group and write the words/ concepts from your list under the various headings. One word may fit under more than one heading. As a group, decide where it is best placed.

How accurate are your perceptions of Queensland? From time to time, as you learn more about Queensland, you will be able to check your original concepts with those learnt during classroom studies of Queensland.

2  What sort of a mental map do you have of Queensland? Try the following exercise without looking at a map.
a  Draw a freehand outline map of Queensland.

b  Now mark in the approximate location of Brisbane, the Gold Coast, Cairns, Townsville, Mt Isa, Birdsville, Fraser Island, the Whitsunday Islands, the Tropic of Capricorn, the Gulf of Carpentaria, the Great Barrier Reef, Daintree National Park.
Check your map against the map, Figure 1.3 How accurate is your mental map?

## Queensland: A comparison with other Australian states

Are Queenslanders different to Australians in other states? What features of Queensland are common to or different from other states? Do you know? This section looks at some factual information about Queensland and compares it with other states.

3  Where is Queensland?
a  Imagine that you are from Mt Isa, travelling overseas and someone asks, 'Where do you live?' Write out a brief but acurate description of the location of Mt Isa.
b  They then say to you, 'Where is Queensland?' Could you give an accurate description of its location? Write out a reply and then check both of your answers against a map.

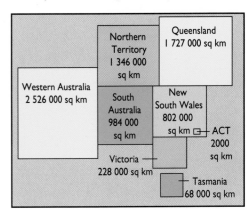

Figure 1.2 The area of the states of Australia

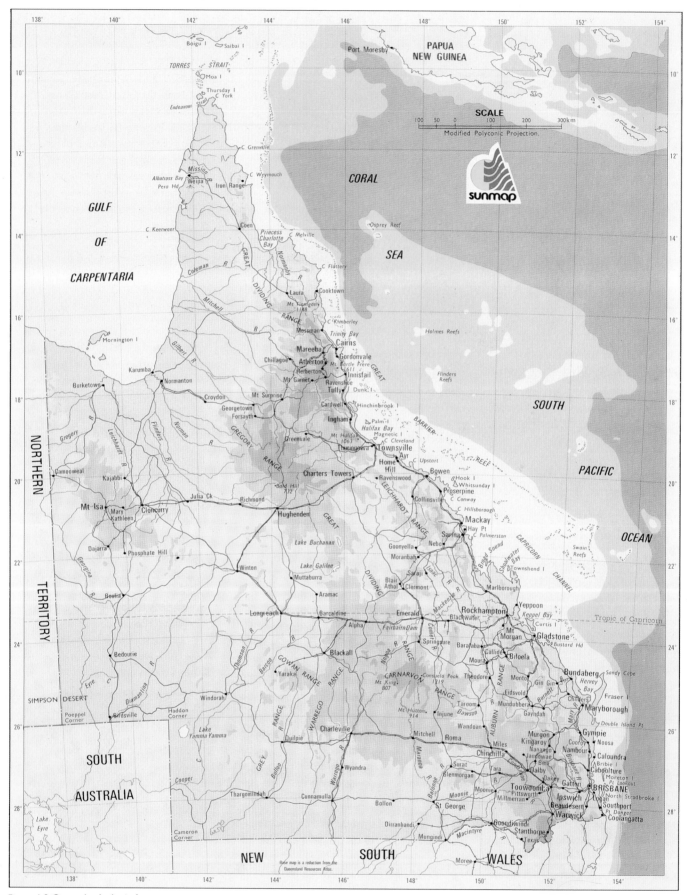

Figure 1.3 Queensland, physical

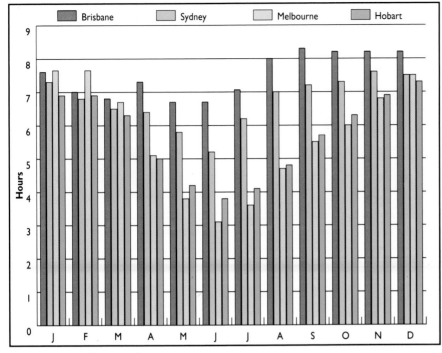

Figure 1.4 Mean daily hours of sunshine

# Cloncurry cooks and Roma shivers with Qld's extremes

## SPECIAL REPORT

The dusty western Queensland town of Cloncurry holds one national record the locals hope it will never set again.

Back on January 16, 1889, the mineral town was smothered in a heat wave which forced the mercury up the scale to 53.1deg—the hottest day recorded in Australia.

Cloncurry's scorcher comes within 5deg of the hottest day recorded on Earth, 58deg at Al'Aziziyah, Libya, on September 3, 1922.

The top three temperatures recorded in Queensland also include Winton (50.7) in December 1888, and Birdsville (49.5) in December 1972.

On Australia Day 52 years ago, Brisbane folk were sweltering through the hottest day recorded in the Sunshine capital on Australia Day, 1940. The temperature reached 43.2deg by mid afternoon.

These are just a sample of the mountain of statistics held in archives by the Bureau of Meteorology since weather patterns were first reliably recorded late last century.

Balmy Queensland figures most prominently in the Australian weather bureau's record books.

Four years after Cloncurry's scorcher, on February 3, 1893, the Sunshine Coast hinterland town of Beerwah was bucketed with the greatest rainfall ever recorded in Australia for a single day—907 mm (36 inches).

The far north Queensland coastal hamlet of Bellenden Ker, near Cairns, boasts the wettest month on record (5387 mm) in January, 1979, and the wettest year, 11,251 mm in 1979.

Babinda, also in the far north, has Australia's highest average annual rainfall of 4537 mm, closely followed by the sugar town of Tully on 4204.

By contrast, Brisbane emerged from a record dry spell in late September last year which lasted 64 days.

Stanthorpe and Warwick are confirmed as Queensland most wintry spots, both recording minimum temperatures below minus 10deg.

Queensland's coldest day was recorded at Stanthorpe on July 4, 1895, when the temperature plunged to a bone-chilling -11deg.

Both Warwick and Stanthorpe recorded temperatures of minus 10.6deg during 1960s.

Brisbane recorded its coldest temperature of 2.3deg on July 14, 1890.

Snow has fallen in several southern Queensland centres, including Roma, the Darling Downs and Brisbane.

Roma residents turned to heavens in astonishment in July, 1960, when light snow fell on their normally hot and dry town.

Snow falls were also reported at Crows Nest in 1901, at Dalby and the Bunya mountains in August 1939 and at Mt Mowbullan on June 10, 1877.

Very light snow has fallen in Brisbane three times this century—on June 28, 1927, in June 1932, and 1958.

The last recorded snowfall in Queensland was at Stanthorpe on July 17, 1989.

Figure 1.5 (The *Courier Mail*, 25 January 1992)

**4** How big is Queensland? Look at the diagram, Figure 1.2.

a What is the area of Queensland in square kilometres?

b What percentage of the total area of Australia does this represent?

c How does Queensland compare in size with other states? Is it the biggest or smallest for example?

d How many kilometres is it, in a straight line, from Brisbane to the tip of Cape York?

e What is the distance from Brisbane to Birdsville?

f Compare the area and extent of Queensland with your own state or, if you live in Queensland, compare it with any other Australian state.

**5** Is Queensland really the 'sunshine state'?

a Look at the column graph, Figure 1.4.

i What does the graph show?

ii Is the evidence on the graph enough to indicate that Queensland is the 'sunshine state'?

iii What other evidence would you find useful to show that Queensland is the 'sunshine state'?

b Queensland's weather, experiences great extremes from time to time. Read the article, Figure 1.5.

i Do any of the weather statistics surprise you? Which ones?

ii How do these extreme weather conditions compare with your local area?

**6** How many people live in Queensland? Look at Table 1.1.

a What is the total population of Queensland?

b In 1990 the population of Australia was 17 086 300. What percentage of the total Australian population live in Queensland?

c Where would you rank Queensland, in terms of population, with other states?

d In 1990 the population of Australia was increasing at a rate of 1.5 per cent. What was the rate of increase in Queensland in the same year?

| Table 1.1 Population statistics, 1990 | | | | |
|---|---|---|---|---|
| State | Population | % of Aust. population | Average annual growth % | Share of growth 1989–90 |
| ACT | 285 000 | 1.7 | 2.26 | 2.5 |
| NSW | 5 827 400 | 34.1 | 0.96 | 21.9 |
| NT | 157 300 | 0.9 | 0.64 | 0.4 |
| Qld | 2 906 800 | 17.0 | 2.57 | 28.7 |
| SA | 1 439 200 | 8.4 | 1.02 | 5.7 |
| Tas. | 456 700 | 2.7 | 1.24 | 2.2 |
| Vic. | 4 380 000 | 25.6 | 1.35 | 23.1 |
| WA | 1 633 900 | 9.6 | 2.46 | 15.5 |
| Aust. | 17 086 300 | 100.00 | 1.56 | 100.00 |

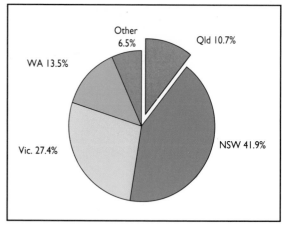

Figure 1.6 Share of overseas settlers 1989–90

e How does this rate of growth compare with other states?

f What do you think could be some of the advantages and disadvantages of an increasing population for Queensland?

**7** Do the people of Queensland have a multicultural background?

a The 1986 census shows the Aboriginal population of Australia as 48 098 people and the Torres Strait Islander population as 13 170 people. Using Figure 1.7 describe the distribution of these peoples. What is Queensland's proportion of the Aboriginal population? Is it more or less than other states?

b The five million people from overseas countries who have settled permanently in Australia since the end of the Second World War have added to a multicultural society. During the 1988–89 period over 163 000 people from overseas countries settled in Australia. Use Figure 1.6 to indicate what Queensland's share was.

c In 1986 approximately 85 per cent of the Queensland population was Queensland born. What other information would you need to give a more accurate picture of a Queenslander?

**8** Is Queensland a highly urbanised state? Australia is a highly urbanised society, with a high percentage of the population living in large cities. Is this also true for Queensland?

a Define an urban area.

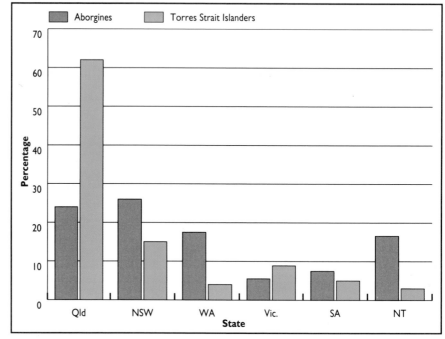

Figure 1.7 Total Aborigine and Torres Strait Islander populations as a percentage in each Australian state

b Does Queensland follow the Australian trend of urbanism?

c How many people live in Brisbane?

d Where does it rank, in size, with other capital cities?

e What percentage of Queensland's population live in Brisbane? Do most of the people in other states live in their capital city?

f Would you say that the population of Queensland is more or less centralised than in other states?

g Are overseas migrants attracted to Brisbane? What further evidence would confirm the pattern shown on the graph, Figure 1.8? Suggest some reasons why most new settlers appear

to be attracted to either Melbourne or Sydney.

h Write a paragraph about the population of Queensland compared with the other states.

| Table 1.2 Capital cities, 1989 | | |
|---|---|---|
| City | Population | % of total state population |
| Adelaide | 1 036 700 | 72.8 |
| Brisbane | 1 272 400 | 45.0 |
| Darwin | 72 000 | 46.6 |
| Hobart | 181 200 | 40.2 |
| Melbourne | 3 039 100 | 70.4 |
| Perth | 1 158 400 | 72.8 |
| Sydney | 3 623 600 | 62.9 |

## Queensland's economic base

The wealth of a country is determined by economic activities such as agriculture, mining, manufacturing, tourism, and so on. The economic performance of a country is indicated by the total wealth produced from all of these activities. The term used for this is gross domestic product or GDP. For Australian states the term used is gross state product or GSP. During the period 1980–81 to 1988–89 Queensland's GSP grew by 142.3 per cent compared with Australia's GDP growth of 137.1 per cent.

---

9 Use Table 1.3.
a What percentage of Queensland's GSP was gained through manufacturing, mining and primary activities in 1988–89?
b How does Queensland's output of each of these three economic activities compare with the total Australian output?

---

For statistical purposes broad general categories of employment are used. Naturally, each category covers a very wide range of specific types of employment. The statistics in Table 1.4 show employment by the type of industry.

### Table 1.3 Queensland's economic base, 1988–89

| Industry | Employment as % of Qld's total | % of GSP | % of Australia's total production |
|---|---|---|---|
| Primary | 6.9 | 6.3 | 21.0 |
| Mining | 1.8 | 6.8 | 24.4 |
| Manufacturing | 11.6 | 13.5 | 11.5 |
| Tertiary | 79.7 | 73.4 | 14.7 |

### Table 1.4 Employment, 1991 Industry

| | Employment as % of Qld's total workforce | Employment as % of Australia's total workforce | Qld employment as % of Australia's total workforce |
|---|---|---|---|
| Primary | 6.8 | 5.4 | 21.2 |
| Mining | 1.6 | 1.3 | 20.0 |
| Manufacturing | 11.5 | 15.6 | 12.5 |
| Tertiary | 80.1 | 77.7 | 46.3 |

---

10 Where do people work in Queensland?
a In which industries are most Queensland people employed?
b Is this employment pattern similar to that for Australia as a whole?
c What types of employment would be classified as tertiary?

---

Do Queenslanders have the same employment opportunities as in other states? The number of people who are available for work are referred to as the workforce. The percentage of the workforce in full-time and part-time employment varies from time to time according to the economy.

---

11 When the most recent unemployment figures are released, find out whether the percentage of unemployed in Queensland is higher or lower than for other states.

---

12 Queensland summary. Use an atlas if necessary to find the answers to these questions.
a Name the three states which share a border with Queensland.
b Name the ocean that borders the east coast.
c Name the two northern neighbouring countries.
d The following words, when unscrambled, will name two each of the items indicated. All are located or grown in Queensland and the names can to be found somewhere in this book.
• Tourist centres:
SCRANI
STUNDIWHAYS
• Rivers:
TAMADIAN
KENIBRU.
• National parks:
YABUN STAIMNOUNS
PEAC BRUILNOATTI
• `Animals:
SCRAWRASOY
GREDHOLEAG RUTTEL
• Minerals:
POPREC
LITRUE
• Crops:
TOTCON
BUNSNAGEM

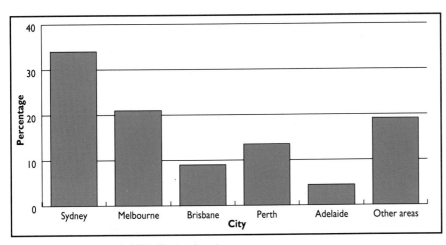

Figure 1.8 Overseas arrivals 1988–89, city of settlement

## Research Topics

Because of the delay between writing and ultimately publishing a book, current information and statistics may, on occasions, vary from that in the text.

### RESEARCH TOPIC 1.1

1. Read the daily newspaper and cut out any information about Queensland. (You may do the same for your own state to compare with Queensland.)
2. File the information, using the same headings as the chapters, and use it as an up-to-date source when studying a particular topic from the text book, or use it in a research topic.

### RESEARCH TOPIC 1.2

A national census, taken every five years in Australia, provides up-to-date information but it takes time for the information to be disseminated to the public. The reason why some 1986 statistics were used in the book is because those from the 1991 census were not readily available at the time of writing. Statistics from the 1991 census (and more recent figures) appear in the media from time to time and are also made available to many local libraries by the Australian Bureau of Statistics.

1. Collect any reference of a statistical nature, from the daily newspapers or magazines, relating to Australia/ Queensland/your own state, (for example, statistics on employment and unemployment, migration population and tourism appear regularly).
2. Check your local library reference section to see what current statistical information is available. Pamphlets of statistics are provided to some local libraries by the Australian Bureau of Statistics.
3. Use these statistics when studying a particular topic to compare with those in the book and see the trend of any changes taking place.

# QUEENSLAND'S NATURAL ENVIRONMENTS

'Queensland is the most naturally diverse state in Australia providing homes for more Australian plants and animal species than any other state or territory'.[1] This diversity of the natural environment is referred to as **biodiversity**. What does it mean? 'Biodiversity is the variety among and within living organisms and the ecological systems in which they occur'.[2]

These natural environments result from the interaction of physical processes, such as climate, landforms, soils, plants and animals, over long periods of time. Some Queensland examples include

- a wet tropical environment
- a coastal environment
- a desert environment.

Can you think of some other examples? The Queensland National Parks and Wildlife Service recognises thirteen mainland biogeographic or natural regions and is developing a park system which reflects and protects this diversity.

---

1 What are the characteristics of some of Queensland's natural environments? Look at the photographs of various Queensland natural environments shown on Figure 2.1.

a What are the main features of the natural environment shown in each photograph?

b Which type of environment do you prefer? Give reasons.

c Do you have any similar environments to those shown in your local area? Which environments?

---

Major landforms generally dominate the landscape and play an important role in determining many of the characteristic features of the natural environment of the region in which they are found. Queensland can be divided into four main landform divisions: the Eastern Highlands, the Western Plains, the North West Uplands and the Coastal Plains. Can you identify these divisions on the map, Figure 1.3?

The Eastern Highlands form part of the range of mountains which is found along the eastern coast of Australia. Millions of years ago, most of this area was submerged by a sea into which large amounts of sediment were

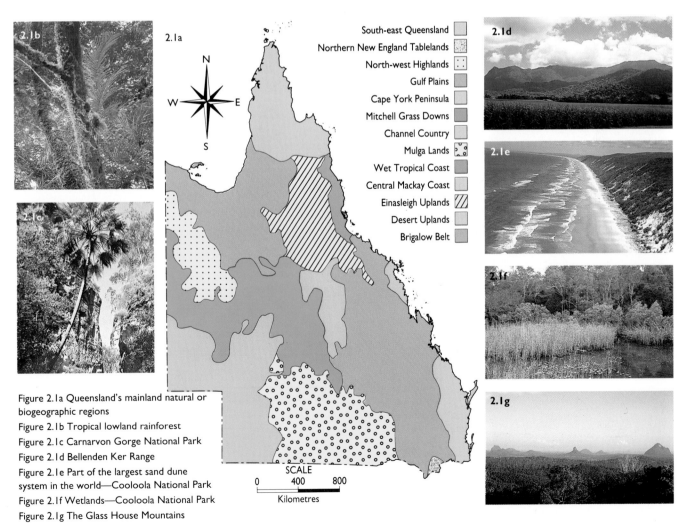

South-east Queensland
Northern New England Tablelands
North-west Highlands
Gulf Plains
Cape York Peninsula
Mitchell Grass Downs
Channel Country
Mulga Lands
Wet Tropical Coast
Central Mackay Coast
Einasleigh Uplands
Desert Uplands
Brigalow Belt

SCALE
0    400    800
Kilometres

Figure 2.1a Queensland's mainland natural or biogeographic regions
Figure 2.1b Tropical lowland rainforest
Figure 2.1c Carnarvon Gorge National Park
Figure 2.1d Bellenden Ker Range
Figure 2.1e Part of the largest sand dune system in the world—Cooloola National Park
Figure 2.1f Wetlands—Cooloola National Park
Figure 2.1g The Glass House Mountains

deposited. Later, earth movements (tectonics) lifted and folded these sedimentary rocks to form the Eastern Highlands. The agents of erosion have been acting on the mountains for millions of years so that, by world standards, they are relatively low in altitude. The highland region consists of diverse landscapes of mountains, plateaus and plains.

Figure 2.2 Queensland landforms

a

b

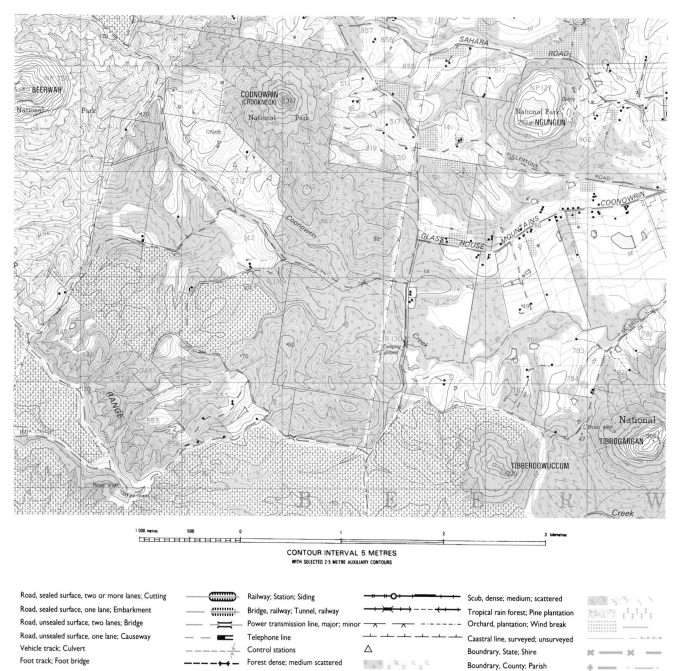

CONTOUR INTERVAL 5 METRES
WITH SELECTED 2·5 METRE AUXILIARY CONTOURS

| | | | | |
|---|---|---|---|---|
| Road, sealed surface, two or more lanes; Cutting | | Railway; Station; Siding | | Scub, dense; medium; scattered |
| Road, sealed surface, one lane; Embankment | | Bridge, railway; Tunnel, railway | | Tropical rain forest; Pine plantation |
| Road, unsealed surface, two lanes; Bridge | | Power transmission line, major; minor | | Orchard, plantation; Wind break |
| Road, unsealed surface, one lane; Causeway | | Telephone line | | Caastral line, surveyed; unsurveyed |
| Vehicle track; Culvert | | Control stations | | Boundary, State; Shire |
| Foot track; Foot bridge | | Forest dense; medium scattered | | Boundary, County; Parish |
| | | | | Name, County; Parish; Portion No. |

Figure 2.3 The Glass House Mountains

WARD ADA 59

**2** Does Queensland have high mountains?

a Using an atlas map locate the Bellenden Ker Ranges. Name the two highest peaks in these ranges. How do they compare in altitude with Mt Kosciusko, Australia's highest mountain?

b Name some other high mountain peaks in Queensland. In which part of the highlands are most high peaks located?

c Although the Eastern Highlands extends almost the whole length of Queensland, it does vary in width. Where is it widest and where is it narrowest?

d Does the range appear to act as a communications barrier between the coast and inland? Give reasons for your answer.

e Do you have mountains in your local area? Where is your nearest high mountain peak? How high is it?

**3** Is there any evidence that volcanic activity played a part in shaping the Eastern Highlands?

a Look at the photographs in Figure 2.2. Describe each landform.

b Look at the topographic map extract, Figure 2.3. Can you identify the landform shown in Figure 2.2a? How high is it? Draw a north–south cross-section from the 100 metre contour line. Use a horizontal scale of 1:25 000 and a vertical scale of 1: 2 500, or you may like to calculate your own scale.

c Name two similar landform features shown on the map and state their height. In what ways are they similar/ different in appearance to the landform feature in Figure 2.2a?

d If you were to walk around the base of these three plugs how far would you walk around each one?

e Can you identify on the map any of the landform features shown on the photograph, Figure 2.1g?

f Make field sketches of both the landforms in Figure 2.2. Suggest how the landforms were formed by referring to the diagrams in Figure 2.4.

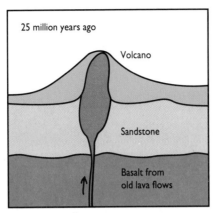

Figure 2.4a Intrusion of magma to form a lava plug

There are many other areas in Queensland which show evidence of past volcanic activity. Some of these include the crater lakes, Barine and Eacham, on the Atherton Tableland and the Undara lava tube system at Mt Surprise in north Queensland.

Do you have any evidence of past volcanic activity in your local area?

**4** Do the Eastern Highlands influence the amount and distribution of rainfall? The general direction for the prevailing winds along the Queensland coast is from the south–east.

a What is the name given to the prevailing wind in Queensland?

b Which of the following would best describe these winds (air masses) when they reach the coast? Give reasons for your choice: warm/moist; warm/dry; cool/moist; cool/dry.

c What effect do you think that these air masses could have on the coast? Look at Table 2.1 showing the average monthly and annual rainfall for various places in Queensland.

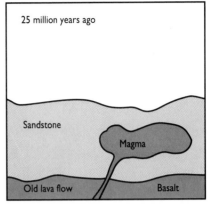

Figure 2.4b The intrusion of magma to form a laccolith

d Describe the average annual rainfall for the places along the east coast. Is there any variation from north to south?

e Look at the places west of the highlands. How does the rainfall differ from that along the east coast?

f Now consider the average monthly distribution of rainfall. Construct a column graph to show the rainfall for the east coast locations in Table 2.1. Use 1mm : 5 mm rainfall for the vertical scale and 1 month : 1cm for the horizontal scale. Shade the four driest months in one colour and the four wettest months in another. Is there a definite pattern of rainfall? Would you describe the rainfall as seasonal? If so, in what months/season does most rain fall?

g Now, construct column graphs for the inland locations, using the same scale as that used for the first graphs. Shade the four driest months and the four wettest months in the same way as the east coast graphs. What major differences in rainfall can you observe between coastal and inland locations?

h One of the wettest places in Queensland is Tully with an average

| Table 2.1 Average monthly and annual rainfall, millimetres | | | | | | | | | | | | | |
| Place | J | F | M | A | M | J | J | A | S | O | N | D | Total |
| --- | --- | --- | --- | --- | --- | --- | --- | --- | --- | --- | --- | --- | --- |
| Brisbane | 161 | 162 | 142 | 88 | 69 | 69 | 55 | 47 | 48 | 74 | 95 | 129 | 1139 |
| Mackay | 261 | 289 | 263 | 112 | 76 | 48 | 20 | 17 | 16 | 33 | 60 | 138 | 1333 |
| Cairns | 401 | 432 | 463 | 170 | 92 | 50 | 30 | 27 | 36 | 33 | 78 | 143 | 1955 |
| Charleville | 73 | 66 | 75 | 34 | 29 | 20 | 23 | 20 | 24 | 41 | 37 | 58 | 500 |
| Longreach | 66 | 85 | 64 | 29 | 23 | 21 | 19 | 9 | 13 | 25 | 28 | 56 | 438 |
| Cloncurry | 90 | 119 | 78 | 22 | 19 | 8 | 6 | 5 | 5 | 14 | 22 | 57 | 445 |

annual rainfall of 4204 millimetres. One of the driest places is Birdsville with an average annual rainfall of 167 millimetres. Locate these places on a map. Can you give some reasons for the amount of rain at each place?

i Do you think that the eastern highlands influence the rainfall? Give your reasons. (Refer to the maps Figure 2.5 and Figure 1.3.)

j Rainfall caused by an air mass crossing a mountain range is termed **orographic**. Do you know the processes involved?

The map, Figure 2.7, was produced from computer analysis of satellite imagery and it was one of the first produced using this technology. It is the most accurate and recent map of Queensland's forests.

Are Queensland's forests all the same? On the map, Queensland's forests are broadly classified as closed forests and open forests. The trees in a forest form a canopy of branches and leaves which act like an umbrella in casting shade onto the forest floor. Where a layered or protective canopy prevents 70 per cent or more direct sunlight reaching the forest floor the term closed forest is used. When more than 70 per cent of sunlight reaches the forest floor the term open forest is used. These broad categories do not show the great diversity and complexity of Queensland's plant communities which represent the evolution of plant species over millions of years.

**5** Has the rainfall distribution influenced the natural vegetation?

a Look at the distribution of forests and woodlands shown on the map, Figure 2.7. Where are the forests located? Does there appear to be a relationship between forests and rainfall?

b What effect does the amount of light falling on the forest floor have on

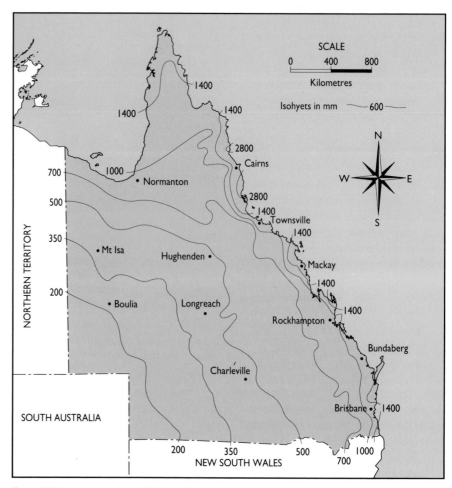

Figure 2.5 Average annual rainfall, Queensland

various plant species? Look at the photographs in Figure 2.6. Which canopy represents a closed forest? Which canopy represents an open forest?

c What other environmental factors, besides rainfall, are important in determining the type of vegetation at a particular place?

What major landform features lie to the west of the Eastern Highlands? West of the mountains and extending to the state boundaries are areas of plains and upland country. The extensive plains which have been built up by material eroded from the highlands cover about two-thirds of the state. The upland area consists of some of the oldest rock formations in the world—the rocks underlying Mt Isa

Figure 2.6 Forest canopy

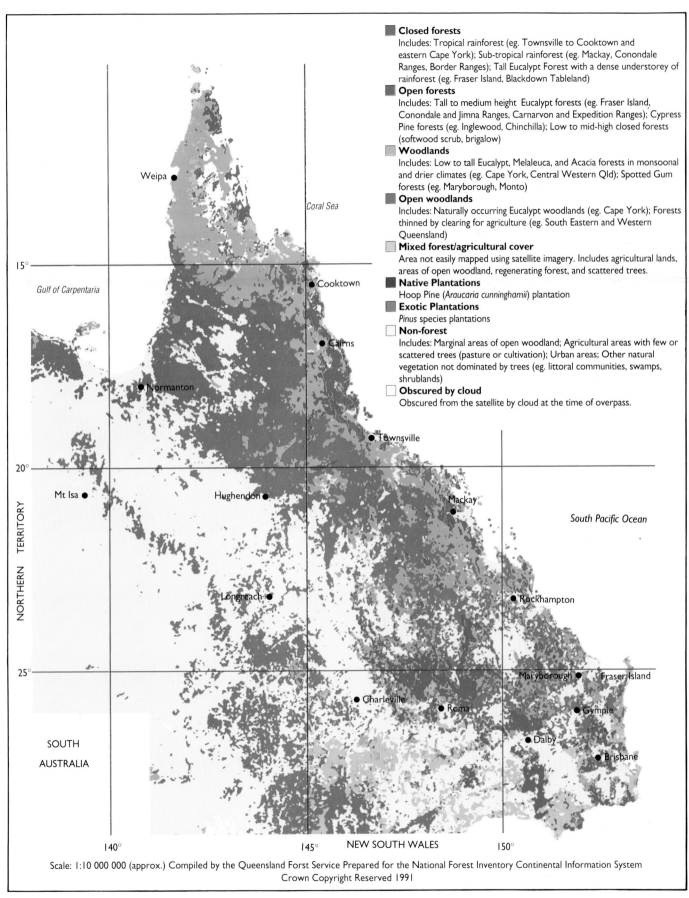

**Closed forests**
Includes: Tropical rainforest (eg. Townsville to Cooktown and eastern Cape York); Sub-tropical rainforest (eg. Mackay, Conondale Ranges, Border Ranges); Tall Eucalypt Forest with a dense understorey of rainforest (eg. Fraser Island, Blackdown Tableland)

**Open forests**
Includes: Tall to medium height Eucalypt forests (eg. Fraser Island, Conondale and Jimna Ranges, Carnarvon and Expedition Ranges); Cypress Pine forests (eg. Inglewood, Chinchilla); Low to mid-high closed forests (softwood scrub, brigalow)

**Woodlands**
Includes: Low to tall Eucalypt, Melaleuca, and Acacia forests in monsoonal and drier climates (eg. Cape York, Central Western Qld); Spotted Gum forests (eg. Maryborough, Monto)

**Open woodlands**
Includes: Naturally occurring Eucalypt woodlands (eg. Cape York); Forests thinned by clearing for agriculture (eg. South Eastern and Western Queensland)

**Mixed forest/agricultural cover**
Area not easily mapped using satellite imagery. Includes agricultural lands, areas of open woodland, regenerating forest, and scattered trees.

**Native Plantations**
Hoop Pine (*Araucaria cunninghamii*) plantation

**Exotic Plantations**
*Pinus* species plantations

**Non-forest**
Includes: Marginal areas of open woodland; Agricultural areas with few or scattered trees (pasture or cultivation); Urban areas; Other natural vegetation not dominated by trees (eg. littoral communities, swamps, shrublands)

**Obscured by cloud**
Obscured from the satellite by cloud at the time of overpass.

Scale: 1:10 000 000 (approx.) Compiled by the Queensland Forst Service Prepared for the National Forest Inventory Continental Information System
Crown Copyright Reserved 1991

Figure 2.7 Forests and woodlands of Queensland

Figure 2.8 The Low Isles, a coral cay on the reef, north-east of Port Douglas

being more than 600 million years old. Vegetation to the west of the ranges has adapted to survive in the lower rainfall. Some examples include bottle trees, brigalow and mulga woodlands, cypress pine forests, and native grasses such as Mitchell and spinifex.

What are the characteristics of Queensland's coastal environments? If you were to travel along the coast of Queensland you would see a great diversity of coastal environments—sandy beaches, rocky headlands, mangroves and, in parts, fertile alluvial plains which have been built up by the coastal rivers. Numerous reefs and islands lie offshore. The islands along the coast have been formed through various processes. Some islands, such as the Whitsundays, were formed by movement of the land (tectonic forces) and changes in sea level (eustatic forces). Some, such as Fraser Island, were formed from deposits of sand, and others, such as the Low Isles, from the action of coral polyps (see Figure 2.8).

**6** Describe the coastal environments shown in the photographs Figures 2.1e and 2.1f.

## Three unique natural environments

The east coast of Queensland has three of the world's most significant natural environments—great sand islands, tropical rainforests, and coral reefs.

### The coastal sand masses

Along the southern coast of Queensland are great sand islands and sand masses, all of which have similar origins. Erosion of the eastern highlands over millions of years provided the rock material which was transported by rivers to the sea. About 20 000 years ago, the sea level was 100 to 200 metres lower than today so the coastline was further to the east and most of the present continental shelf was dry land. The rock particles (sand) were picked up and carried inland by the south-east prevailing winds to form massive sand dunes. Later, with the rise in sea level, the present coastline formed and these sand masses are the ancient dunes now in the centre of the islands. Sediments and sand, carried along the coast by ocean currents and waves, continue to build up and maintain the beaches by a process of longshore transportation. Sand picked up from the beach maintains the present dune system. These sand dune islands are unique and in some cases have important habitats which evolved because the islands were isolated from the mainland.

Fraser Island is the world's largest sand island. Fraser Island has a unique lake system as well as a wide variety of plant communities, one of the most significant being the satinay forests. The species, satinay or Fraser Island turpentine (*Syncarpia hillii*), is almost exclusively limited to Fraser Island

with a few stands on the mainland at Cooloola.

### The tropical rainforests

The Queensland rainforests can be divided into two broad groups. The sub-tropical rainforests of southern Queensland and the wet tropical rainforests further north. They both provide an important link with the past and the historic evolution of plants over a period of 130 million years, from the time Australia was part of the continent of Gondwanaland to the present day. 'The Queensland rainforest is one of the most breathtakingly wild

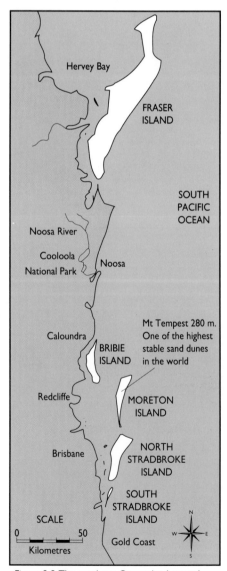

Figure 2.9 The southern Queensland coastal sand masses

areas in the world; unbelievably beautiful, unbelievably interesting. There are birds, mammals, and plants there that are unique. Beyond any dispute it is a treasure.'[3] These are the words of the world-famous naturalist, David Attenborough.

## The coral reefs

The Great Barrier Reef is a unique natural environment and it is considered to be the largest structure on earth created by living creatures. It stretches about 2000 kilometres along the east coast of Australia. However, it is not one continuous reef but consists of thousands of offshore reefs and fringing reefs along its length. Although covering an area of about 343 880 square kilometres, only about one tenth of the region is occupied by coral reefs.

## Protection of unique environments

Over the last two decades these three areas—Fraser Island, the wet tropical rainforests of northern Queensland and the Great Barrier Reef—have been the subject of bitter conflict between people with different viewpoints on how the natural resources should best be used. The reef and parts of the northern rainforests are now protected by being placed on the World Heritage List. Fraser Island will soon be included. The World Heritage List is a register of areas of outstanding cultural or natural value and through the listing the areas are assured of protection for future generations. Can you name other World Heritage areas already listed in Australia?

## The changing natural environment

All natural environments are susceptible to change. Natural events and physical processes which lead to environmental change differ from time to time and place to place and occur on a variety of scales. Change may be rapid, slow, short or long term.

One example of long term change is the evolution of the schlerophyll flora which replaced the tropical rainforest over much of Australia. This change was associated with a period of global cooling and a more arid climate. The remnants of the ancient forests of Gondwanaland survived only in small areas as eucalypts and other plant species became dominant.

Bushfires are a natural part of the Australian environment. Wet sclerophyll forests, which contain a mixture of both eucalypt trees and rainforest trees, illustrate how the natural environment can change over time. Rainforest trees are very sensitive to fire, being unable to withstand intense heat because of their thin bark. Eucalypts are insensitive to fire, in fact fire helps in regeneration. After a fire eucalypts quickly regenerate from buds in the trunk. Fire also encourages seeding. So the regular occurrence of natural fires in wet sclerophyll forests keeps the rainforest plants in check and encourages eucalypts to grow. Without fire the rainforest species would dominate and eucalypts would find it harder to regenerate on the shadier forest floor. Transition from eucalypt to rainforest or from rainforest to eucalypt therefore occurs subject to the frequency and intensity of fire.

The natural environment shows a remarkable capacity to recover from natural disturbances. The changes that may take place illustrate the dynamic nature of the environment. For example, a coral reef is a delicate and fragile ecosystem. Natural agencies such as cyclonic storms, excessive sedimentation from rivers, prolonged emersion at low tide and biological agencies, such as fish, crabs, starfish and other organisms, can damage sections of the reef. However, the reef has a remarkable ability to repair damage caused by these natural occurrences.

## Change brought about by human activity

The Aborigines used fire as a management tool and in doing so

---

**RESEARCH TOPIC 2.1**

Choose either Fraser Island, the wet tropical rainforests of north Queensland or the Great Barrier Reef.

a Show the location/distribution on a map.

b Describe the main characteristics of the environment. Use diagrams, sketches and brief notes. Outline processes involved in the development.

c Explain how the area was utilised in the past by the Aborigines and the effect that human activities have had on the area since European settlement.

d Outline the steps taken to preserve the area. Was there conflict between people? What were the major issues and how were they resolved?

e How is the area managed today?

f What problems are faced in protecting the area for future generations?

indirectly controlled the spatial limits of the rainforests in some areas. Their use of fire also created and maintained areas of grassland which were so attractive to the early European pastoralists. Because of their special relationship with the environment over thousands of years, the Aborigines developed a sustainable balance between people and the environment.

However European settlement was the beginning of vast changes to and, in some areas, the complete destruction of, the natural environment. European settlers came from places where, over a period of more than a thousand years, most of the natural environment had been replaced by a rural landscape. Their attitude to land was to modify the natural environment to make it productive and so improve it. They could not understand the Aboriginal attitude to the land nor why so few people needed such large areas for their subsistence.

---

7 Do you know why a hunting and food gathering society needs a relatively large area of land? Discuss.

---

As settlements spread throughout Queensland large areas of the natural environment were either destroyed or modified to create the 'human' or 'built' environment in which we live today. The expansion of rural and urban areas has resulted in many species of plants and animals becoming extinct or endangered as their habitats are destroyed.

# Turtles could 'disappear from Qld in 10 years'

## By DANIELLE KOOPMAN

Loggerhead turtles could disappear from the southern Queensland coast in five to 10 years, a researcher said yesterday.

Greenpeace researcher Mr Trevor Daly said urgent action had to be taken to save the turtles which had become a major tourist attraction.

"It is very important Queensland looks after its population. The turtles are a big tourist drawcard and important to the local economy," Mr Daly said.

Bundaberg District Tourism and Development Board manager Mr Paul Neville said the disappearance of the turtles would have a "serious effect" on tourism and local economy.

"It does for Queensland tourism what the fairy penguins do for Phillip Island," he said. "They are an important part of Bundaberg's tourism."

Mr Neville said it was difficult to quantify the importance of the turtle and was seeking more information on the threat of disappearance.

The loggerhead turtle is one of six sea turtle species in Australia—all are threatened with extinction.

Mr Daly said many were killed in trawler nets and crab traps or in collisions with speedboats.

Mr Daly was a researcher in a Queensland National Parks and Wildlife Service survey of south-east Queensland nesting beaches, including the internationally-renowned Mon Repos beach near Bundaberg.

"These are the largest and most important rookeries for this species in the entire Pacific Ocean region," he said.

"Over the last 10 years the number of female loggerhead turtles coming ashore to nest at the beaches has been declining but it has become particularly serious over the last five nesting seasons.

"During last year's season, which just ended, only 170 females nested compared with approximately 290 in 1985 and over 400 in the late 70s."

Mr Daly said if the numbers continued to drop at the present rate the population could disappear from the southern Queensland coast in five to 10 years.

He called on the State Government to ban all trawling off Mon Repos during the nesting season, increase research funds, declare the proposed Woongarra Marine Park off the beach before next summer and implement a tourist crowd control plan before the nesting season.

"The sheer numbers of tourists attempting to view the turtles at Mon Repos is getting out of control," Mr Daly said.

Regional manager of Fisheries in south-east Queensland Dr John Glaister said the Environment and Primary Industries departments had agreed on a plan to investigate the problem and calculate numbers being caught in trawlers.

"It is a legitimate concern and we are quite aware there may be problems in the Bundaberg area," he said.

A Primary Industries Department spokesman said no action would be taken until a further one-year study was carried out by Dr Colin Limpus beginning in July.

Figure 2.10 (The *Courier-Mail*, 10 April 1990)

---

## RESEARCH TOPIC 2.2

Some of Queensland's endangered species include the northern hairy-nosed wombat, the bridled nail-tailed wallaby, the brush-tailed bettong, the greater bilby, and the golden-shouldered parrot. Some endangered marine species include the dugong, flatback turtle, and the leathery turtle. Choose one from the list (or you may prefer to choose a species not listed above). It is better if class members choose different species and then discuss them after completing the research.

a  Show the present and former distribution of your chosen species on a sketch map.

b  Describe its habitat.

c  Outline the changes taking place which have endangered the species.

d  Explain what attempts are being made to preserve the species.

## The introduction of exotic species

In an attempt to modify and improve on nature, and for other reasons, many exotic plants and animals were introduced into Queensland. By upsetting the balance of nature, these plants and animals in many cases have had a detrimental effect on the natural environment and its plant and animal life. The prickly pear (which looks like a huge cactus) can still be seen growing in parts of Queensland. However, in Figure 2.11 you can read about the problems it caused before it was brought under control. The introduced cane toad is rapidly spreading throughout Queensland and even beyond the borders. Feral animals, such as the pig, are also a severe problem as the article in Figure 2.12 indicates.

## Queensland's natural hazards

A hazard involves a degree of risk, uncertainty and the element of chance. Riding a bicycle along a busy road is a hazard. How can you ride along the busy road and make the journey less hazardous? What risks do you face? Extreme natural events such as tropical cyclones and floods occur from time to time as part of various global processes. These extreme natural events can be seen as potential hazards because it is not known exactly when they will occur or how severe they will be.

What is a natural hazard? A natural hazard exists where there is interaction between people and the natural environment. Whenever we experience extreme natural events, during which property is damaged and perhaps lives are lost, we refer to them as natural disasters.

## Reclamation of prickly pear lands

Prickly pears, which are natives of North and South America, were brought into Australia in the early days of colonisation.

Several kinds of pears became noxious weeds, but the two related species, the common pest pear, *Opuntia inermis*, and the spiny pest pear, *Opuntia stricta*, increased and spread to such a degree as to overrun very large areas of good pastoral lands.

Prickly pear was disseminated either by seed or by segments, every one of which was liable to take root even after considerable exposure or immersion. The main distribution was by seeds which passed through the digestive systems of birds or animals that had eaten the pulpy fruit.

The magnitude and seriousness of the problem are shown by the rate of spread of the pest. In 1900 an estimated area of 4m hectares was affected and by 1925, when the peak of the invasion was reached, more than 24m hectares were affected. About half of this area represented heavy infestation. Fences were buried beneath the plants and settlers waged a ceaseless but oft-times losing battle—digging, crushing, burning, poisoning and pulling out by the roots.

Both chemical and biological methods of destruction were investigated, but none of the chemical methods was economical for other than scattered infestations. In 1920 the Commonwealth Prickly Pear Board was established. Officers of the Board commenced investigations in 1921 and studied cactus insects in North and South America for 16 years. It was not only necessary to ensure that insects were capable of the destruction of the pear, but that they were unable to live on the plants of economic value.

The eventual victor, *Cactoblastis cactorum*, was imported and bred at a newly constructed laboratory at Sherwood. The first liberations of this insect were made in 1926—2,263,150 eggs in 19 localities (14 in Queensland and 5 in New South Wales). Within 15 months after the first trial, many large plants of prickly pear had been destroyed. By 1933 the last big area of the original pear was destroyed by the insect. As the pear decreased, so did the population of *Cactoblastis*. For a time it was thought that regrowth would occur and flourish, but the *Cactoblastis* recovered and attacked the regrowth.

The work of *Cactoblastis cactorum* against prickly pear is still continued. In dry years, prickly pear tends to make regrowth, sometimes enough to worry the owners of properties into believing that the pear is again taking over. The *Cactoblastis* however multiplies again, particularly in wet years, but there is usually a 5 year lag in the ability of the insect to cope with the regrowth.

Figure 2.11 (*Queensland Year Book, 1989*)

## North plans war on forest-killing pigs

**A legacy to the nation by Captain Cook—pigs carried on the Endeavour escaping into the far north Queensland forests—is causing increasing alarm... since hunting was banned after World Heritage listing three years ago, feral pigs have increasingly threatened forests by destroying the understorey plants. FRANK SANDERSON reports:**

Feral pigs which are taking over the far north Queensland rainforests are under fire as they threaten disaster for the World Heritage area.

Chairman of the Hinchinbrook Shire Council, Cr Rea Brown, based at Ingham, believes the feral pig problem must be confronted immediately.

There is no time to wait for a management plan for the forests to be finalised, which could take two years he says.

The whole forest under-storey and the ground-living birds—scrub turkeys and cassowaries—are at risk as the pigs build up towards plague proportions.

Under-storey plants die or are ripped out and eaten as the soil of the forest floor is rooted up by pigs travelling in herds.

The pigs also have been blamed for stirring up and spreading a pathogen from the soil, suspected of causing a fatal disease affecting victims who had been working in their gardens last wet season.

Cr Brown believes that unless the pig plague is wiped out, there will be no rainforest because no young trees can survive.

Eventually the rain forest will die and become a wasteland.

He says the pig population will continue to increase unless professional shooters are allowed in.

"I am not aware of any accredited people being allowed into the forest but there must be action soon on this," he said.

Farmers in the Milla Milla area report that pigs come out of the rainforest to damage farm crops; and in lower areas severe cane crop damage has been reported.

In several rainforest sections near the Abergowrie Forestry Reserve—a pine plantation—in the Hinchinbrook Shire, the soil looked as if it had been worked with a rotary hoe.

Nothing was left growing where pigs had foraged for roots, small plants, fallen figs and other fruit; nearby, wallows had been formed in a small mountain stream.

A Tully resident said he had seen up to 40 feral pigs in one herd, most of them young, foraging in and near a forest area creek.

Cr Brown said the damage done by the pigs was a cause for concern to anyone who valued the rain forest.

A former member of an advisory committee on World Heritage matters, he said he had warned consistently about the potential for disaster as the feral pig numbers grew.

He said forest authorities would have to employ skilled hunters with well trained pig dogs.

There was little use in taking poorly trained dogs into the forest and widespread baiting would not be acceptable to the community.

"The community and councils are aware there is a problem in the forests and urgent action is essential," he said.

The Johnstone Shire council, based at Innisfail, has agreed to build three prototype pig traps for a local group fearful of the damage pigs are doing to the cassowary population at Mission Beach.

Figure 2.12 (The *Sunday Mail*, 13 October 1991)

**8** Think about natural hazards.

a Can you name at least four extreme natural events which could be perceived as potential hazards?

b Do you have natural hazards in your local area?

c Name two natural disasters which have taken place in Queensland in recent years.

## Tropical cyclones

Each year Queensland coastal communities face the threat of one or more of the greatest storms on earth—tropical cyclones. Tropical cyclones are an integral part of the general circulation of the atmosphere and occur in various parts of the world. They are also called typhoons or hurricanes.

Tropical cyclones which may affect Queensland coastal areas usually develop in the Coral Sea, Solomon Sea, or the Gulf of Carpentaria.

## Case study: The stormy life of tropical cyclone 'Joy'

On 15 December 1990 a tropical low pressure system developed over the ocean north-east of Queensland. Two days later it had deepened to below 1000 hectopascals and was moving in a south-west direction. This was the beginning of a tropical cyclone which was code-named 'Joy'. TC Joy was to become one of the biggest threats to coastal populations for many years.

**Table 2.2 Monthly occurrence of tropical cyclones in Queensland, 1909-91**

| Month | Number |
|---|---|
| December | 34 |
| January | 95 |
| February | 96 |
| March | 87 |
| April | 44 |
| Other months | 30 |
| **Total** | **386** |

**9** Use Figure 2.25 (p.27) to help you answer this question.

a Where do tropical cyclones occur in Queensland?

b Which parts of Queensland appear to be most at risk from a cyclone?

c During which months do most tropical cyclones occur?

d What is the average number of cyclones a year for each of these months?

**10** Track TC Joy.

a Where was the tropical depression located on 18 December? Calculate its approximate distance from Cairns using Figure 2.14a.

b Meteorologists track cyclones using weather satellites, radar and automatic weather stations located on coasts and islands. Weather observers, as well as ships captains and commercial aircraft pilots in the vicinity, also contribute. Photocopy the cyclone tracking map, Figure 2.13, and using the track data in Table 2.3 plot the course of TC Joy.

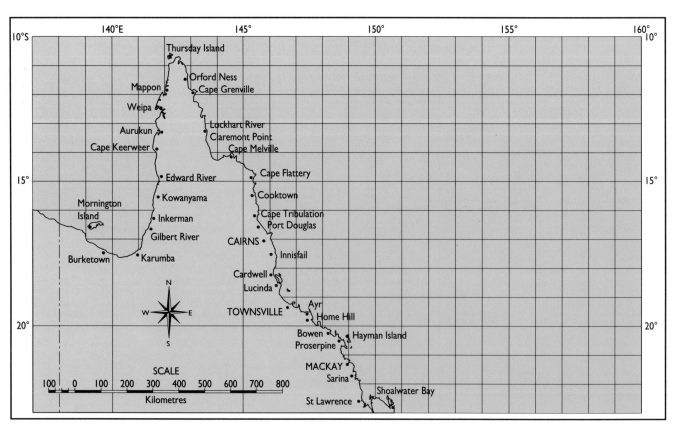

Figure 2.13 Cyclone tracking map

A tropical low west of the Solomon Islands was moving slowly south-west but had not shown any significant signs of significant development. A strong wind warning was current for East Coast waters between Cooktown and Bustard Head.

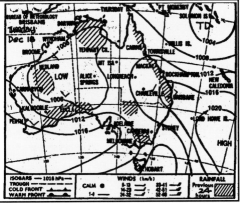

a

Sunday evening tropical cyclone Joy was almost stationary about 120 kms north-east of Cairns. Moderate to heavy rain and strong winds were being reported from the far north coast. Most of the rest of the State has continued to experience dry weather with above normal temperatures. The greatest departures from normal have been in the south-east corner with temperatures yesterday up to 11 degrees above normal. This has been due to a very warm and stable atmosphere ahead of a trough moving into western Queensland. In southern Queensland, the atmosphere is slightly more unstable and some thunderstorms have been generated late in the day. A seasonal monsoon flow is established over Cape York Peninsula and some thunderstorms have occurred.

b

Tropical cyclone Joy at 6pm was crossing the coast near Ayr. Rain and squally winds were being experienced on the coast between Ingham and St Lawrence with the worst conditions between Townsville and Mackay. The rain extends inland to the central highlands and southward to the Curtis district but in other south-eastern districts only isolated showers occurred, though skies were overcast. A fresh monsoon flow established across Cape York Peninsula with thunderstorms occurring on the Peninsula and around the Gulf. A trough lies across the interior from near Mt Isa to the Cunnamulla area. There have been isolated thunderstorms near the trough but fine weather has prevailed elsewhere in the west of the state.

c

The system which was tropical cyclone Joy has degenerated into a rain depression and yesterday afternoon was located near Charters Towers and moving further south. A high in the north Tasman Sea extends a weak ridge on to the southern Queensland coast and this, with rain depression, produced wet, windy weather about the central coast. Rain areas had extended inland to the central highlands and southwards into the northern Curtis region by Thursday evening. The inland trough had moved rapidly west recently and is not considered a significant feature at this stage. A fresh monsoon flow is well established across Cape York Peninsula with associated thunderstorm activity occurring on the Peninsula and around the Gulf. A deep low over Victoria has an associated trough extending to central Australia

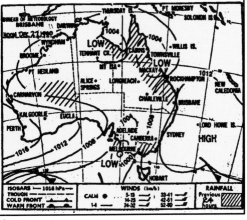

d

Figure 2.14 Weather maps

c Describe the course and calculate the distance travelled by TC Joy.

d Draw a line graph to show the variation in air pressure as TC Joy increased and decreased in intensity. ( A horizontal scale of 1 cm : 1 day and a vertical scale of 1cm : 10 hPa could be used or you may calculate your own scale. Choose the same time for each day on the horizontal scale.) Mark on the graph significant stages in the life of TC Joy as you continue this exercise.

e Look at the satellite image of TC Joy shown in Figure 2.15 and the map Figure 2.14b. Draw a sketch of the cyclone. Mark in the eye of the cyclone and use arrows to show the direction of the wind. Mark in the approximate wind speed at various parts of the cyclone. How far was TC Joy from Cairns at this stage?

f How big is the cyclone? Calculate the approximate east–west and north –west diameters of the cyclone. Mark these measurements on your sketch.

g Where and when did TC Joy eventually cross the coast?

What is significant about a cyclone crossing the coast? It is when a cyclone makes landfall that the full force of its energy is unleashed on any community that happens to be located there. Strong winds and heavy rainfall may also be accompanied by a storm surge. The force of the wind drives the water forward as a huge wave which acts like a giant bulldozer, sweeping over the land, eroding the coastline, damaging property and inundating low lying areas. Over 90 per cent of the world's deaths from tropical cyclones this century have been caused by storm surges.

Storm surges associated with tropical cyclones also occur along Queensland's coast. In 1989 a storm surge of up to 3 metres in Upstart Bay, near Ayr, north Queensland, was caused by TC Aivu. All buildings along the beachfront were

Figure 2.15 Tropical cyclone Joy

destroyed and one person was drowned. Storm surges are greater if they coincide with a period of high tide.

Why do tropical cyclones die? The energy of a cyclone develops over the warm ocean waters. As soon as the cyclone hits land the built-up energy is rapidly dissipated and the cyclone dies to become a low pressure area, referred to as a rain depression.

---

11 Aftermath of TC Joy.

a Were any high tides predicted during TC Joy?

b What eventually happened to TC Joy? (See Figure 2.14d.)

c What aspects of the movement of TC Joy could cause concern for coastal communities?

**Table 2.3 Tropical cyclone Joy, December 1990: Best track data at 3 hourly intervals**

| Date | Time | Latitude ° south | Longitude ° east | Central pressure | Date | Time | Latitude ° south | Longitude ° east | Central pressure | Date | Time | Latitude ° south | Longitude ° east | Central pressure |
|---|---|---|---|---|---|---|---|---|---|---|---|---|---|---|
| 18 | 1100 | 11.5 | 158.0 | 998 | 22 | 0500 | 14.6 | 148.1 | 965 | 25 | 2000 | 17.3 | 147.9 | 980 |
| 18 | 1400 | 11.8 | 157.6 | 998 | 22 | 0800 | 14.9 | 147.9 | 965 | 25 | 2300 | 17.3 | 147.9 | 980 |
| 18 | 1700 | 12.1 | 157.2 | 998 | 22 | 1100 | 15.0 | 147.6 | 960 | 26 | 0200 | 17.5 | 147.9 | 980 |
| 18 | 2000 | 12.4 | 156.7 | 998 | 22 | 1400 | 15.2 | 147.4 | 960 | 26 | 0500 | 17.8 | 147.9 | 980 |
| 19 | 2300 | 12.7 | 156.3 | 995 | 22 | 1700 | 15.2 | 147.4 | 955 | 26 | 0800 | 18.0 | 147.9 | 980 |
| 19 | 0200 | 12.9 | 155.7 | 995 | 22 | 2000 | 15.5 | 147.5 | 955 | 26 | 1100 | 18.3 | 147.9 | 980 |
| 19 | 0500 | 13.1 | 155.1 | 995 | 22 | 2300 | 15.4 | 147.2 | 950 | 26 | 1500 | 18.9 | 147.7 | 980 |
| 19 | 1100 | 12.3 | 153.3 | 990 | 23 | 0200 | 15.8 | 147.2 | 945 | 26 | 1700 | 19.3 | 147.6 | 983 |
| 19 | 1400 | 12.3 | 153.0 | 990 | 23 | 0500 | 16.0 | 146.9 | 945 | 26 | 2000 | 19.2 | 147.3 | 990 |
| 19 | 1700 | 12.3 | 152.7 | 985 | 23 | 0800 | 16.1 | 146.8 | 945 | 26 | 2300 | 19.2 | 147.1 | 990 |
| 19 | 2000 | 12.4 | 152.5 | 985 | 23 | 1100 | 16.0 | 146.7 | 940 | 27 | 0200 | 19.2 | 146.9 | 990 |
| 19 | 2300 | 12.5 | 152.5 | 985 | 23 | 1400 | 16.1 | 146.7 | 940 | 27 | 0500 | 19.3 | 146.6 | 992 |
| 20 | 0200 | 12.5 | 151.9 | 985 | 23 | 1700 | 16.3 | 146.7 | 940 | 27 | 0900 | 19.9 | 146.5 | 997 |
| 20 | 0500 | 12.5 | 151.6 | 985 | 23 | 2000 | 16.2 | 146.6 | 940 | 27 | 1200 | 20.0 | 146.7 | 999 |
| 20 | 0800 | 12.5 | 151.3 | 980 | 23 | 2300 | 16.2 | 146.6 | 940 | 27 | 1500 | 20.1 | 146.9 | 999 |
| 20 | 1100 | 12.5 | 151.0 | 970 | 24 | 0200 | 16.2 | 146.7 | 940 | 27 | 1800 | 20.2 | 146.8 | 999 |
| 20 | 1400 | 12.5 | 150.8 | 970 | 24 | 0500 | 16.3 | 146.8 | 940 | 27 | 2100 | 20.3 | 146.6 | 999 |
| 20 | 1700 | 12.6 | 150.6 | 970 | 24 | 0800 | 16.4 | 146.8 | 940 | 27 | 2400 | 20.5 | 146.8 | 999 |
| 20 | 2000 | 12.7 | 150.3 | 970 | 24 | 1100 | 16.7 | 146.7 | 950 | 28 | 0300 | 20.5 | 147.2 | 999 |
| 20 | 2300 | 12.8 | 150.1 | 970 | 24 | 1400 | 16.7 | 146.8 | 950 | 28 | 0600 | 20.4 | 147.3 | 999 |
| 21 | 0200 | 12.9 | 149.8 | 970 | 24 | 1700 | 16.7 | 146.9 | 950 | 28 | 0900 | 20.4 | 147.4 | 999 |
| 21 | 0500 | 13.0 | 149.6 | 970 | 24 | 2000 | 16.6 | 147.1 | 955 | 28 | 1200 | 20.3 | 147.6 | 999 |
| 21 | 0800 | 13.1 | 149.3 | 970 | 24 | 2300 | 16.7 | 147.2 | 955 | 28 | 1500 | 20.3 | 147.8 | 999 |
| 21 | 1100 | 13.3 | 149.1 | 970 | 25 | 0200 | 16.8 | 147.1 | 970 | 28 | 1800 | 20.3 | 147.8 | 999 |
| 21 | 1400 | 13.5 | 148.9 | 970 | 25 | 0500 | 16.9 | 147.2 | 970 | 28 | 2100 | 20.4 | 147.4 | 999 |
| 21 | 1700 | 13.8 | 148.8 | 970 | 25 | 0800 | 17.0 | 147.2 | 975 | 28 | 2400 | 20.5 | 147.7 | 999 |
| 21 | 2000 | 14.1 | 148.6 | 970 | 25 | 1100 | 17.0 | 147.5 | 975 | 29 | 0300 | 20.6 | 147.6 | 1000 |
| 21 | 2300 | 14.3 | 148.4 | 965 | 25 | 1400 | 17.1 | 147.7 | 980 | Landfall occurred near Cape Bowling Green/Alva | | | | |
| 22 | 0200 | 14.6 | 148.1 | 965 | 25 | 1700 | 17.2 | 147.8 | 980 | | | | | |

d   Do all tropical cyclones follow an unpredictable course?

e   Can you imagine what your feelings would be if you were in a coastal community with TC Joy hovering offshore? What would be a major cause of stress?

---

What was the impact of Joy on the various settlements? The total damages bill for Joy was estimated at $300 million! Here are some brief details

- extensive damage to crops, buildings, powerlines, etc.
- widespread flooding resulted from the heavy rainfalls which exceeded 2000 millimetres in places—Mackay received 1830 millimetres
- six people died from drowning in the aftermath of TC Joy.
- power failures also ensued— retailers lost hundreds of thousands of dollars of stock as refrigerators ceased to operate.
- banana crops were flattened by 150 kilometre per hour winds
- thousands of tourists were stranded as airports closed
- fruit was stripped off mango trees and thousands of macadamia nut trees were blown over on the Atherton Tablelands
- gale force winds lashed the north Queensland coast
- trees were uprooted, houses were un-roofed
- many cane fields were flattened
- maize and peanut farmers seemed to be the only ones who were pleased with widespread rain.

---

**12** Using information from what you have learned about TC Joy, write a journalist's report for a local newspaper. Above your report write your own headline similar to the three following examples.

'Sugar loss could reach $2m' (The Cairns Post)

'Storms cost big retailers dearly' (The Cairns Post)

'Joy blitzes Mackay with $40m. damage bill' (The Courier Mail)

---

The economic cost of a cyclone can be relatively easily calculated, but what about the social cost? Many people quickly revert to their normal life after a cyclone but others may need counselling and other assistance. The effect of tropical cyclones such as Tracy (Darwin, 1974) can be traumatic for many people.

## Cyclones and the natural environment

Cyclones are a natural phenomenon and although they inflict damage it is just part of the on-going changing nature of the natural environment. For example, destruction to part of a forest permits light to fall on the forest floor encouraging growth of a variety of plant species. Vegetation killed by the tropical cyclone soon decays and contributes to the nutrient cycle.

But what about habitats? The environment of a specific animal or bird is usually referred to as its habitat.

The degree of risk attached to an extreme natural event and the extent to which it may damage or disrupt a settlement is related to the extent to which people are able to adjust to their environment. Since we have no control over tropical cyclones, how can the risk of loss of life and damage to property be reduced?

# Reef corals killed by Cyclone Joy's deluge

### By BRIAN WILLIAMS
### environment reporter

About 85 percent of shallow water corals in the Capricorn section of the Great Barrier Reef have been killed by fresh water dumped by Cyclone Joy.

All the territorial fish which inhabited the reefs have also been killed.

The cyclone flooded Rockhampton at the start of the year. The Fitzroy River pushed millions of tonnes of fresh water out as far as the Capricorn Group of islands, about 100km off Rockhampton in central Queensland.

The head of research at the great Barrier Reef Marine Park Authority, Mr Simon Woodley, said yesterday corals down to about 1.5 m below the surface had been killed.

A second band of coral down to about 2m had been severely stressed.

"When this occurs, the corals spit out the algae which lives in the tissue," Mr Woodley said.

"This gives the coral a bleak or bleached white look."

Mr Woodley said coral had been killed by the lack of salinity in the water and the amount of sediment.

The fish killed had been mainly the territorial "pretty" species. Populations were static for those species which had moved away from the affected reefs.

Mr Woodley said the reefs most damaged were those on the western side of the islands in the Bunker group, Capricorn Group and Keppel Group.

Researchers expected the coral species would recolonise in about five to seven years.

The reefs would not be nearly as attractive but he did not expect any untoward effects on tourism and sufficient funds were not available for researchers to establish exactly how large an area had been affected.

"Most of the operators prefer to go further out for coral viewing because of turbidity closer in," Mr Woodley said.

The dead corals were being overgrown already by algae and weeds.

Reefs off seven islands had been surveyed by James Cook University, Townsville, researchers.

Coral had also been killed between Hamilton and Dent Islands in the Whitsunday passage to the north, Mr Woodley said.

This natural phenomenon had also been recorded in 1918 and 1954.

A survey of Magnetic Island would be taken this month and a further survey to check for damage and regrowth would be taken in about 12 months.

Figure 2.16 (The *Courier-Mail*, 25 June, 1991)

The Bureau of Meteorology, through Tropical Cyclone Warning Centres (TCWC), monitors tropical cyclones which may develop. The Bureau then issues warnings to threatened communities. Advice messages are sent to all radio and television stations in the threatened area, as well as to local police, government bodies, State Emergency Services and others. If a cyclone exists but there is no threat to coastal communities within twenty-four hours, a cyclone *watch* is issued. As soon as indications are that gale force winds will affect coastal communities within twenty-four hours, a cyclone *warning* is issued. The estimated intensity of a cyclone is included in the report.

13 Look at Table 2.4.
a What scale of intensity is used?
b What was the greatest intensity of TC Joy? When?

During TC Joy the TCWC in Brisbane issued ninety-eight public watches and warnings. The first watch was issued at noon on 19 December, the first warning was issued at 8 am on 21 December, and the final advice was issued at 10 pm on 26 December. This was the greatest number of advices issued for any cyclone in Australia (see Figure 2.17).

14 Analyse the warnings.
a What do the terms watch, warning and advice mean?
b What information do the warnings contain?
c How do you think this information could assist you if you were living in a cyclone area?

What can people do to reduce the hazard of a tropical cyclone?

---

### THE FIRST WARNING FOR THE CAIRNS REGION

TROPICAL CYCLONE ADVICE NUMBER 9 ISSUED BY THE BUREAU OF METEOROLOGY BRISBANE AT 8 AM EDST FRIDAY 21 DECEMBER.

A TROPICAL CYCLONE WARNING IS NOW CURRENT FOR COASTAL AND ISLAND COMMUNITIES BETWEEN CAPE MELVILLE AND INNISFAIL.

A TROPICAL CYCLONE WATCH EXTENDS NORTHWARDS TO LOCKHART RIVER AND SOUTHWARD TO TOWNSVILLE.

TROPICAL CYCLONE JOY, CATEGORY 2, IS ABOUT 490 KILOMETRES EAST-NORTHEAST OF COOKTOWN AND MOVING WEST-SOUTHWEST AT 12 KILOMETRES PER HOUR.

GALES WILL DEVELOP BY TONIGHT ON THE OUTER ISLANDS BETWEEN CAPE MELVILLE AND PORT DOUGLAS AND EXTEND ONTO THE COAST EARLY SATURDAY.

FLOOD RAINS MAY DEVELOP IN COASTAL STREAMS BETWEEN INGHAM AND COOKTOWN TONIGHT.

DETAILS OF TROPICAL CYCLONE JOY, CATEGORY 2, AT 8AM

CENTRAL PRESSURE: 973 HECTOPASCALS

LOCATION OF CENTRE: WITHIN 60 KILOMETRES OF LATITUDE 13.5 DEGREES SOUTH LONGITUDE 148.7 DEGREES EAST ABOUT 490 KILOMETRES EAST-NORTHEAST OF COOKTOWN

CURRENT MOVEMENT: WSW AT 12 KILOMETRES FROM THE CENTRE

MAXIMUM WIND GUSTS: 150 KILOMETRES PER HOUR NEAR THE CENTRE

THE NEXT ADVICE WILL BE ISSUED AT 11AM.

Figure 2.17a

---

### SEVERE TROPICAL CYCLONE JOY UPGRADED TO CATEGORY 4

TROPICAL CYCLONE ADVICE NUMBER 32 ISSUED BY THE BUREAU OF METEOROLOGY BRISBANE AT 9AM EDST SUNDAY 23 DECEMBER.

A TROPICAL CYCLONE WARNING IS CURRENT FOR COASTAL AND ISLAND COMMUNITIES BETWEEN COOKTOWN AND TOWNSVILLE.

SEVERE TROPICAL CYCLONE JOY, UPGRADED TO CATEGORY 4, HAD A VERY DESTRUCTIVE CORE WITH WIND GUSTS TO 230KM/H NEAR THE CENTRE. 'JOY' IS MOVING SLOWING SOUTHWEST TOWARDS THE COAST.

DESTRUCTIVE WINDS ARE BEING EXPERIENCED ALONG THE EXPOSED COAST BETWEEN COOKTOWN AND INNISFAIL AND COULD EXTEND SOUTH TO LUCINDA DURING THE DAY.

FLOOD RAINS ARE EXPECTED IN COASTAL STREAMS BETWEEN COOKTOWN AND INGHAM DURING THE DAY.

TIDES BETWEEN COOKTOWN AND LUCINDA ARE LIKELY TO RISE UP TO 2.0 METRES ABOVE NORMAL DURING THE DAY, SEA LEVELS MAY EXCEED HIGH WATER MARK WITH VERY ROUGH SEAS AND FLOODING OVER THE FORESHORE.

DETAILS OF SEVERE TROPICAL CYCLONE JOY, CATEGORY 4, AT 9AM

CENTRAL PRESSURE: 940 HECTOPASCALS

LOCATION OF CENTRE: WITHIN 40 KILOMETRES OF LATITUDE 16.1 DEGREES SOUTH LONGITUDE 146.7 DEGREES EAST ABOUT 180 KILOMETRES EAST-SOUTHEAST OF COOKTOWN AND 135 KILOMETRES NORTHWEST OF CAIRNS

RECENT MOVEMENT: SOUTHWEST AT 7KM/HR

DESTRUCTIVE WINDS: OUT TO 140 KILOMETRES FROM THE CENTRE

MAXIMUM WIND GUSTS: 230 KILOMETRES PER HOUR NEAR THE CENTRE

THE VERY DESTRUCTIVE CORE OF 'JOY' IS POSING A MAJOR THREAT TO COMMUNITIES BETWEEN COOKTOWN AND LUCINDA.

RESIDENTS ARE ADVISED TO SHELTER IN A SAFE PLACE FOR THE DURATION OF THE DANGEROUS CONDITIONS.

THE NEXT ADVICE WILL BE ISSUED AT 10AM.

Figure 2.17b

---

| Table 2.4 Cyclone severity categories | | | | |
|---|---|---|---|---|
| Category | Average wind (km/h) | Strongest gust (km/h) | Central pressure (hPa) | Typical effects (indicative only) |
| 1 | 63–90 | Less than 125 | Greater than 985 | Negligible house damage. Damage to some crops, trees, caravans. Craft may drag moorings. |
| 2 | 90–120 | 125–170 | 985–970 | Minor house damage. Significant damage to signs, trees, caravans. Heavy damage to crops. Risk of power failure. Small craft may break moorings. |
| 3 | 120–160 | 170–225 | 970–945 | Some roof and structural damage. Some caravans destroyed. Power failures likely. |
| 4 | 160–200 | 225–280 | 945–920 | Significant roofing loss and structural damage. Many caravans destroyed and blown away. Dangerous airborne debris. Widespread power failures. |
| 5 | More than 200 | More than 280 | Below 920 | Extremely dangerous with widespread destruction. |

Although cyclones are a natural hazard the people of Queensland are able to live in reasonable safety because local authorities have strict building codes for cyclone areas so that buildings are less likely to be damaged. People are kept well informed of the location, intensity and predicted movement of cyclones.

15 What else can individuals do to minimise the risks? Discuss.

## Rainfall: Too much or too little?

The rainfall of Queensland shows great variability, not only from year to year but from place to place in the same year. This unreliable pattern of rainfall results in all or in part of the state being subject to flood or drought conditions at some time.

During the years 1990 and 1991 Queensland communities faced both widespread flooding and severe droughts. Almost the whole of Queensland was affected in one way or another and many parts of the state were declared natural disaster areas.

16 Look at the map, Figure 2.18.
a Describe the pattern of surface runoff shown for the various drainage divisions.
b What do you think would be the major differences in the flow of the rivers to the east coast, inland and to the Gulf? Give reasons.
c Do you think that the flow of rivers would be seasonal? If so, when and why?
d Which mountains act as a divide or watershed between the Gulf of Carpentaria and the Lake Eyre divisions? (See Figure 1.3 also.)
e Into which river system do the rivers of the south mid-west region flow? Where do they discharge into the ocean?

f Where do the waters of the Lake Eyre division flow?
g Using an atlas, trace the river system in the Lake Eyre division to its destination in South Australia. This river system is known as a basin of internal drainage. What does the term mean? What do you know about the physical features and climate of the area into which these rivers flow? What would happen to much of the water carried by the rivers in this system?

## Floods

A flood is a natural characteristic of rivers and can be defined as a discharge of water in excess of normal channel capacity. Periodic flooding is a common phenomenon in most drainage basins and can occur on a variety of scales ranging from a small local stream flooding to one covering a major drainage system. Floods generally result from a major increase in the water input

into the system, usually climatically controlled, such as heavier than average or unseasonal precipitation or a severe local thunderstorm or tropical cyclone.

Although many river systems have regular or seasonal flood periods, flooding may occur at any time. Since river flood plains are important areas for human settlement, floods are seen as a natural hazard. Widespread flooding usually leads to loss of livestock and damage to property in both rural and urban areas.

After severe flooding in western Queensland in April 1990, widespread and heavy rainfall early in 1991 resulted in further severe flooding over most of the state.

17 Answer the following questions.
a What two natural events may lead to the flooding of Queensland's rivers?
b Most Queensland floods occur in the months of January to April. Why?

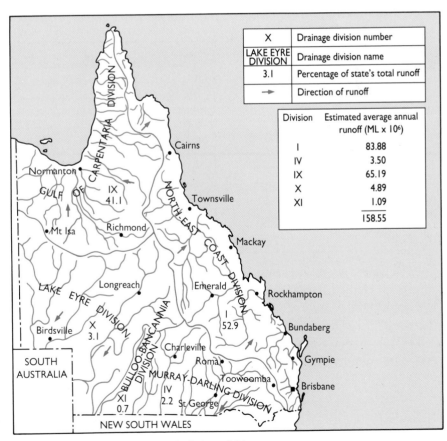

Figure 2.18 Rainfall runoff distribution by drainage division

Between December 1990 and February 1991 the northern tropical coast experienced one of the wettest seasons on record and flooding of coastal streams between Cairns and Townsville was almost continuous during that period. Many communities faced some of the worst flooding in living memory. Rockhampton had its worst floods in thirty-seven years and the Fitzroy River reached a record peak of 9.3 metres on 12 January. Many properties were isolated and major transport links were cut by flood waters.

The Ayr and Home Hill areas also experienced very heavy rainfall and the flooding of the Burdekin River resulted in widespread damage to both communities and sugar cane crops. Other communities along the coast also experienced widespread flooding.

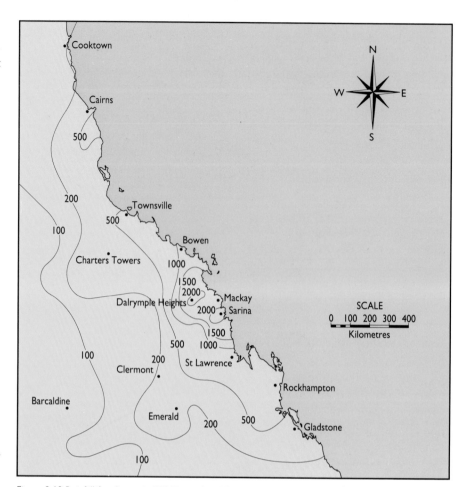

Figure 2.19 Rainfall for the period 23 December 1990 to 7 January 1991

**18** Look at the map, Figure 2.19.

a Which parts of the coast experienced the heaviest rainfall during the time period shown?

b How do the rainfall totals for this sixteen day period compare with average January rainfalls for Rockhampton (159 millimetres), Townsville (307 millimetres) and Cairns (399 millimetres)?

c Check the location of Ingham. How much rain fell over the Ingham area during this time period?

d What is the average rainfall for Ingham for these months?

Heavy rain fell on the catchment area of the Herbert River from late December 1990 to the end of February 1991. The Herbert River had previously peaked below minor flood levels around 25 December 1990.

**19** Look at Figure 2.20. Gairloch is the location of a stream gauging station.

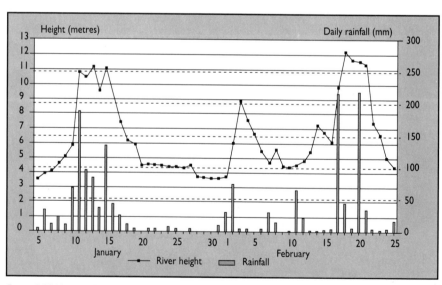

Figure 2.20 Herbert River at Gairloch, January–February 1991 floods

a On how many days during the period shown did rain fall?

b On which days were the highest rainfalls and how much rain fell?

c How many times did the river peak and what were the highest peak flood levels during this period?

d Suggest reasons why the river peaked so rapidly after the onset of the higher rainfall days.

e What happened to the river flow as the rain eased after 17 January and again on both 3 February and 21 February?

# ONGOING FLOODS JUST BAD LUCK, SAY WEATHER EXPERTS

## By John Wright

Even by Queensland standards, it has been a bad run.

Ever since Cyclone Nancy whipped down the coast a year ago, drenching the Gold Coast and northern New South Wales, it has been a case of floods, floods and more floods. At least that's how it seems.

After Nancy it was the Big Wet in Charleville and some other unlucky western towns—the worst floods in 100 years, locals said. Then it was Rockhampton and Mackay, soaked by Cyclone Joy and its aftermath last month, and then most of northern and western Queensland flooded by monsoon rains and still swimming.

And now it is Boonah and Dugandan, Rathdowney and Kooralbyn, in the south-east of the state, cut off or inundated by yet more floods. Is there some significance here—dramatic global warming, maybe, or the celebrated El Nino effect gone berserk?

The short answer is that while Queensland has been very wet in the past 12 months, the floods have had more to do with bad luck than with extraordinary deviations from normal weather patterns.

The Weather Bureau says recent heavy rain in the south of the state and the flash floods yesterday in Boonah, Rathdowney and Dugandan is associated with a southern drift of the monsoonal system.

Cyclone Nancy in southern Queensland and two others (Greg and Ivor) which followed it in north Queensland in March last year were nothing exceptional in a state accustomed to seasonal cyclones.

The outback floods which devastated Charleville and other towns just a month later were a different matter, though meteorological opinion is that extraordinary changes to weather patterns were not to blame.

The first hint the state had that something abnormal was about to happen came in mid-April when the weather bureau started giving flood warnings for distant inland rivers which flowed through the great expanses of south-western Queensland and into northern New South Wales.

In the space of just over two weeks, the central-west catchment areas of the inland's major rivers were inundated by what meteorologists described as "rainfall events" which gave some inland centres 10 times their average rainfall figure.

The first two saturated the catchments; the third and largest of the three fell on April 10. The rain it dumped had nowhere to go but down the already swollen river courses, turning a vast area of central and southern Queensland into a lake and causing the worst floods in a century.

The Great Wet prompted speculation that it had been caused by a sudden reversal or collapse of the drought-producing El Nino weather phenomenon, or its opposite, La Nina. Brisbane Weather Bureau meteorologist Barry Gordon does not subscribe to this view.

"There are very natural variations in weather, and we can get extremes, be it drought or floods," he said yesterday.

If central western Queensland was unlucky in April with that last fall of rain, so too was north Queensland a few months later with Cyclone Joy.

The bad luck this time for the north and central coastal districts was that Cyclone Joy—an unusually wet cyclone by meteorological standards—had barely dissipated last month when it was followed by heavy monsoonal rains.

Again—as was the case with the central west floods in April—the latest rain fell on to catchments already saturated. Rivers which had peaked and begun to subside in Joy's aftermath started to rise again, and even now are expected to pose more flooding threats to Rockhampton.

All this is not to say that the past 12 months in Queensland have been unusual. For many, they have been not only devastating but heartbreaking. For others, they have meant countless hours of unpaid and often dangerous work in combating the forces of nature.

State Counter Disaster Organisation and SES operations officer Henry Christie said the past 12 months had seen the most intensive period of SES activity he'd seen in years.

"Very few of the 35,000 SES volunteers in the state would have missed out on active work in the past 12 months," he said. "It started in the south-east corner with Nancy and now it's come full circle with the latest floods.

"Now Rockhampton is rearing its ugly head again and expecting another flood peak and Giru is going under again right now. This office (the disaster organisation's operations room) has been manned non-stop since December 15 for up to 24 hours a day. We've coped very well as far as resources go, though it has obviously cost taxpayers a great deal of money."

The Insurance Council of Australia's regional manager, Mr Graham Jones, described the 13 months since the Newcastle earthquake as "one period of chaos after another" in Queensland and New South Wales.

"It's been fairly costly as far as storm damage and flooding goes...certainly the worst for many years," he said yesterday. "The (insurance) claims worked out at $1 million to $2 million for each of the cyclones early last year and more than $30 million for the April floods.

"The figures for Cyclone Joy are still being worked out...A rough estimate would be $15-$20 million. The actual damage bill is many times more than the amount in claims."

The total damage bill may never be accurately assessed. The cost to the State Government can.

Disaster relief payouts under the Commonwealth State agreement have been estimated at more than $128 million since Cyclone Nancy, of which the State Government has had to find $58 million from a rapidly emptying barrel.

A spokesman for the Premier, Mr Goss, said the string of natural disasters had placed a "greater and greater strain" on the State's ability to pay for the damage, even accounting for the Commonwealth's disaster relief contributions.

The spokesman said: "It's not driving the State broke, but it will mean a recasting of the Budget projections.

"The money has to come from somewhere to pay these damages bills and thus meet the State's obligations. It has to come out of other programs."

During the Herbert River floods two-thirds of the town of Ingham was inundated by water up to 5 metres deep. Parts of the main street were under two metres of water. More than one hundred and fifty people were evacuated from their homes. For the people of Ingham this was the third highest flood on record.

The following extract, from a Bureau of Meteorology flood report issued in February 1991, details inland floods of north, central and western Queensland.

*Major flooding continued throughout February in the Flinders and Cloncurry Rivers with many towns and properties remaining isolated. Emergency food and fodder resupply operations continued throughout February...*

*Further rain during early February over most of central and western Queensland saw major flooding develop in most inland river systems... Major flooding developed in the Paroo and Bulloo Rivers with the Paroo River at Eulo peaking at 5.4 metres on 8 February, the fourth highest flood on record...*

*In the Thomson River major flooding occurred during early February with flooding extending down to the Cooper Creek during mid-February. Windorah peaked at 6.7 metres on 11 February, with flooding extending downstream of Windorah over the following weeks...*

*Major flooding also developed in the Diamantina and Georgina Rivers, with Birdsville peaking at 8.2 metres on 25 February. Widespread flooding and traffic difficulties continued throughout February in these areas with many towns isolated...*

---

**20** Using an atlas, locate all the rivers and towns referred to in the report.

a   In what ways are inland river floods different to those of the coastal rivers? Give your reason. (See also Figure 2.25.)

b   Even though widespread rains had not fallen in south-west Queensland some areas were flooded. Can you explain why?

c   What caused such widespread floods throughout Queensland during these months? (See Figure 2.21.)

Figure 2.21 (The *Courier-Mail*, 9 January 1991)

## AUSTRALIA DAY FLOODS

The most extensive floods on recorded history to affect Queensland as a whole occurred during January 1974...

It is probably fortunate that the trough produced only two cyclones during the month, Vera which formed in the Coral Sea on 19 January 1974, and subsequently moved south east and Wanda which formed on 23 January. The southerly movement of Wanda and trough extended the heavy flooding to south-east Queensland at the end of the month...

Peak totals for the month were reported from the south-east coastal ranges with figures near 2,000 millimetres and in one instance 2,300 millimetres and it was this rainfall which led to disastrous floods by the end of January 1974.

Because of its greater population density, the most severely affected area in terms of financial loss was the south-east corner of Queensland. The inundation over the inland caused lengthy road and rail dislocation and heavy stock losses. In the north west and west of the State the major streams remained above major flood level until mid-February.

In the Brisbane-Ipswich area the main floods commenced with local flash-flooding in the metropolitan creeks. Over the period 25 to 27 January flash floods occurred registering record levels in the Enoggera, Moggill, Bundamba, Woogaroo and Oxley Creeks and Kedron Brook while all other creeks recorded major flooding. Although these floods were damaging to property immediately surrounding the creek banks, they were over-shadowed by later flooding of the Brisbane River and record flooding of the Bremer River.

On the basis of recordings taken at the Brisbane Port Office, the main Brisbane River flooding commenced after 8 a.m. on Saturday, 26 January 1974, reached its peak of 6.59 metres about 2 a.m. on 29 January 1974, and receded below flood level by 9 p.m. on 30 January 1974. During this period some 6,700 householders in the Brisbane area had their living area either partially or totally inundated and about as many properties again reported the land or foundations affected. Some houses were washed away in the creek flooding and others collapsed into the Brisbane River.

Record flash-flooding of the creeks combined with the Bremer River produced record flood levels in Ipswich, where approximately 40 houses were washed away and 1,800 premises severely damaged from the resulting high run-off and backwater from the Brisbane River...

The estimated damage in and around Brisbane alone was $200m and 15 lives were lost in south-east Queensland.

Figure 2.22 (*Queensland Year Book*, 1989)

Flash flooding usually occurs when a drainage system cannot quickly and efficiently carry away the water runoff following a severe storm. Flooding of this nature is usually sudden and short-lived but can cause extensive damage, especially when it occurs in an urban area.

One of the most severe flash floods in Queensland's history occurred on 26 January 1974 and is referred to as the Australia Day floods (see Figure 2.22).

**21** Read Figure 2.22.
a What caused the heavy rainfall that led to the flooding?
b How long did the Brisbane flooding last?
c Suggest reasons why urban areas often experience flash flooding.
d Which parts of Queensland are subject to flash flooding?
e Have you experienced flash flooding in your area? If so, describe what happened.

The Bureau of Meteorology advises communities, through Flood Warning Centres, as soon as a potential flood threat develops. The warnings are aimed at reducing the social and economic impact of flooding. Through the use of radio telemetry, rainfall and river level information is automatically recorded and transmitted by radio links to a receiving station. The severity of the potential flood can be calculated and local agencies alerted. Flood warnings are usually stated as minor, moderate or major. The Bureau issued 132 flood warnings in January 1991 and another 345 in February.

Flood control can also be achieved by the construction of storage dams, so that water from floods can be contained and released without damage at a later date.

**22** What are some of the problems associated with such schemes for the western Queensland rivers? Discuss.

## Droughts

Droughts are part of the Australian environment, and a reminder of the unreliability or variability of rainfall. An extensive drought affected almost the whole of eastern Australia in 1982–83, but less than a decade later, in 1991–92, many parts of Queensland suffered from the longest drought on record.

Drought is difficult to define but one definition is a 'lack of sufficient water to meet normal requirements', and another definition is a 'serious deficiency of rainfall'. Definitions will vary from place to place as people have different concepts of a drought. For many Queensland urban dwellers, drought may simply mean the inconvenience of having water restrictions—when the use of water for hosing gardens, washing cars and other uses is restricted by local or state, water authorities.

**23** Read the definitions in the paragraph above.
a What do you think is wrong with these definitions?
b Write down what you think is a reasonable definition of a drought.
c Is drought only a matter of personal inconvenience for urban dwellers? Try to think of all the ways in which a drought can have an indirect impact on urban dwellers. The following headlines, taken from the Queensland newspaper the *Courier Mail*, may help.
'Barbeques will be banned if state stays dry'
'Water bans as dams dry up'
'Farmers see fields turned into dustbowls'
'Farmers to get drought funds'
'Dalby water restrictions for the first time in 30 years'
'Drought forces costs up, production down"
'Big dry to cost state $750 million—Goss'
'Pineapple supplies dry up in drought'
'Drought hits cane crop for 2nd year'

For people in the rural areas of Queensland who rely on farming or pastoral activities for their livelihood, a drought can be a disaster. In January 1991, about one-third of Queensland's primary properties were drought declared. The drought affected about half the sheep grazing country and one-third of the cattle country. The most severely affected parts were Mitchell, Charleville, Tambo, Quilpie and Cunamulla, as well as Longreach and the Julia Creek regions.

---

**24** Discuss the effects that a drought may have on a farming family and a farm community. Refer to both economic and social effects.

---

A drought usually starts after a dry period, when pastures are almost depleted and water storage levels fall. This is the time when people realise that a drought is upon them. A drought usually finishes after widespread rain falls, indicating that a more normal pattern of weather can be expected to follow. However, for some communities the drought can be broken in a less than welcome fashion. Sometimes drought-breaking rain can lead to extensive flooding. In February 1992 good rainfalls were recorded in the far west and north Queensland regions, but heavy rain, caused by a slow moving tropical low, led to extensive flooding in south-east Queensland. People who had applied for drought relief were quickly requesting flood relief! After two days of extremely heavy rainfall, the towns of Maryborough and Gympie were flooded and the Sunshine Coast recorded the two wettest days on record. In a period of twenty-four hours Tewantin received 732 millimetres of rain, Yandina 668 millimetres, Mt Coolum 532 millimetres and Mapelton 513 millimetres. Have you ever experienced rainfall such as this in your area?

What action can be taken to diminish the effects of a drought? The Bureau of Meteorology, through its National Climate Centre, monitors the weather and issues monthly

'Drought Statements' until rainfall deficiencies are removed, usually following widespread rains. Each Drought Statement contains maps, like the example in Figure 2.23, as well as other information.

---

**25** Look at Figure 2.23.
a   What categories are used to indicate the degree of rainfall deficiency?
b   Describe the pattern of rainfall deficiency for Queensland during the period shown.

---

Drought researchers are also attempting to develop an early warning system using data related to soil type, stock numbers, the amount of pasture, and kangaroo

numbers. Further research into what causes a drought is also being conducted.

The question of what does cause a drought is complex. Queensland's rainfall is part of the global system of climate which is a very complex interaction of the physical elements of the atmosphere, the oceans, the biosphere and the polar ice masses. In recent years scientists have identified certain variations in the global climate system which they refer to as the El Nino Southern Oscillation or 'El Nino' for short. Recent research indicates that the current drought in Queensland may be the result of this global phenomenon(see Figure 2.24).

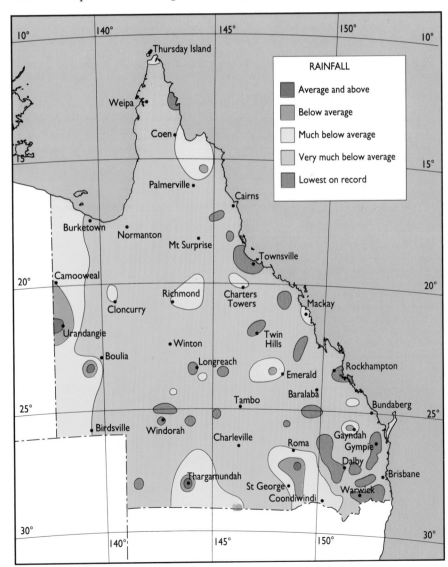

Figure 2.23 Drought monitoring, 1 March to 30 November 1991

## Bushfires

Every year Queensland is subject to periodic bushfires and the threat of bushfire is often statewide. Generally, the peak danger season is late in the year after good rains have encouraged thick growth and before the arrival of the wet season. Because of the severe drought in 1991 the fire hazard in the south-west of Queensland was very intense.

**26** Think about the bushfires.

a Unlike the south-east of Australia, the hottest period of the year in Queensland is not necessarily the worst fire danger period. Why?

b When is the peak bushfire danger period in your locality?

c What conditions make your area prone to a potential bushfire risk?

d In what ways do people increase the risk of a bushfire?

## Earthquakes

People in Australia were shocked with the reports of the Newcastle earthquake of 1989. The earthquake, which registered 5.6 on the Richter scale, killed twelve people. Before the Newcastle incident many people thought that earthquakes only occurred in other countries. But can an earthquake happen in Queensland?

**27** Look at the map, Figure 2.25.

a Describe the distribution of earthquakes in Queensland.

b Where are the greatest risk zones?

## Can sunshine be a natural hazard?

The warm, sunny climate of Queensland is envied by many people who live further south. Pictures of suntanned bodies on beautiful Queensland beaches are prominently displayed in glossy tourist brochures. But can Queensland have too much sunshine? The temperature of a place is influenced by its latitudinal position, distance from the coast and altitude.

**28** How warm is Queensland's climate?

a Compare the range of temperatures between January and July for the places shown in Table 2.5.

b Which places have the greatest range of temperatures inland/coastal, north/south?

c Do average monthly temperatures differ from north to south and from east to west?

d How do the average monthly temperatures compare with those where you live?

e Which of the following best describes Queensland's temperature, in general terms? You may use more than one : tropical, sub-tropical, warm temperate, cool temperate, cold. Do you think latitude, distance from the coast or altitude are important in determining the temperature of the places referred to in Table 2.5? Give reasons.

f What is the latitudinal extent of Queensland?

g Approximately how much of Queensland's total area lies north of the Tropic of Capricorn?

The Tropic of Capricorn is a line marked on maps to indicate the

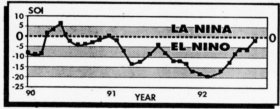

# The wet's on the way but will it El Nino out, La Nina in

Scientific indications are that Queensland's weather is hovering at the edge of recovery from the El Nino episode that has plagued it with drought for the past two years.

The Southern Oscillation index (SOI) graph that depicts atmospheric pressure trends over the Pacific has almost reached the dividing line between the rain-inhibiting El Nino and rain-producing La Nina .

A weather indication report issued by the Brisbane Weather Bureau for the next three months says some computer models suggest the weather is heading into a La Nina episode, but the indications at this stage are by no means clear.

The report says there is an indication that some useful rainfall is likely in some areas of Queensland between now and the end of December.

It says SOI readings point to the possibility of an earlier-than-usual monsoon onset over northern Australia and an approximately average number of tropical cyclones.

Queensland averages four or five cyclones over its offshore waters each cyclone season.

Rainfall over the next three months is likely to be at least average over the north-west and south-east parts of the continent.

Figure 2.24 (The *Courier Mail*, 11 October, 1992)

### RESEARCH TOPIC 2.3

a Is El Nino the cause of drought in Australia? What is El Nino? Where does it occur?

b What processes are involved in the El Nino phenomenon? How frequently does it occur?

c What changes in normal weather patterns occur as a result of El Nino?

d How does El Nino influence the weather of Queensland, Australia, and other Pacific Rim countries?

e What indicators are scientists using in an attempt to monitor the possibility of an El Nino occurring?

f What can be done to lessen the impact of El Nino in Australia?

g What is La Nina?

southern limit of the sun being directly overhead of a place at solar noon (midday).

In the southern hemisphere this occurs on 22 December and is referred to as the southern summer solstice. The heating power of the sun is greatest at this time. (The sun is overhead at the Tropic of Capricorn on 22 June—this is the time of the northern summer solstice.)

The amount of solar energy reaching the earth's surface is termed 'insolation'. The quantity of insolation received at a place in one day depends on

- the angle at which the sun's rays strike the earth—this is related to the latitudinal position of a place, so places nearest to the equator receive more direct sun rays than places towards the poles
- the length of time of exposure to the sun's rays—this is determined by the season, for example hours of daylight are usually longer in summer than in winter and in general, insolation is greatest between the hours of 11 am and 3 pm (standard time).

**29** Answer the following questions.
a At what times of the year is the sun directly over the equator at noon?
b How many times each year would the sun be overhead at noon at Cairns, Rockhampton, Brisbane? Give reasons for your answers.

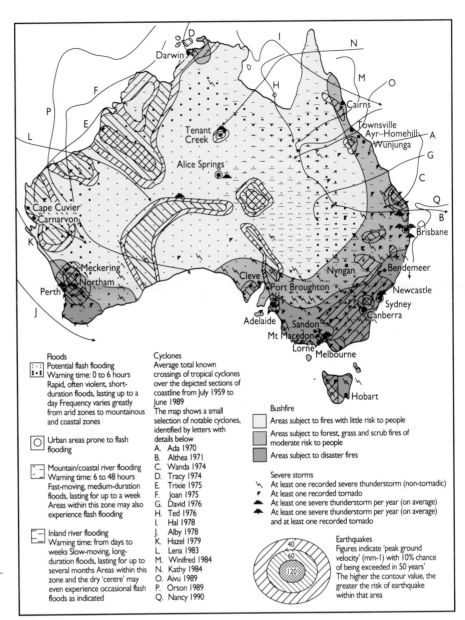

Figure 2.25 Australia's natural hazard zones

| Table 2.5 Average daily maximum temperatures, °C | | |
| --- | --- | --- |
| Place | January | July |
| Brisbane | 31.4 | 23.5 |
| Cairns | 31.5 | 25.4 |
| Charleville | 34.6 | 21.7 |
| Cloncurry | 37.8 | 27.7 |
| Longreach | 37.9 | 23.3 |
| Mackay | 30.6 | 23.0 |

**RESEARCH TOPIC 2.4**

a How did Australia and the other southern continents evolve to their present shape? Describe the location of the various plates.
b Is there a relationship between earthquakes and the movement of continents? Where are the major earthquake zones of the world?
c Name the plate on which Australia is located. In what direction is it moving and how fast?
d Which countries are located on the northern boundary of the plate? Is there evidence of earthquake/volcanic activity in those countries?
e Where are the major earthquake zones in Australia? These areas are not on plate boundaries so what is the main cause of earthquakes in Australia?
f What is an earthquake? How is it measured?
g What is the effect of an earthquake on the natural environment? What is the effect on people?
h How can a community reduce the hazard of an earthquake?
i Can earthquakes be predicted? What research is being carried out in an attempt to predict earthquakes?

Figure 2.26 A skin cancer warning, the Gold Coast

Exposure to too much sunshine without adequate protection for the body increases the risk of skin cancer. Skin cancer can result in death. The rapid increase in the number of Queensland people suffering from skin cancer is making people more alert to the fact that too much sunshine is a health hazard. An article in *The Medical Journal of Australia* [4] states that Queensland has the highest incidence rate for non-melanoma skin cancer in the world. It also confirms the relationship between latitude and lifestyle. Of the four areas surveyed, north Queensland had higher rates than Brisbane and the Darling Downs. The Gold Coast, although at a similar latitude to Brisbane, showed rates similar to those of north Queensland.

**30** Can you suggest some reasons for differences in the areas surveyed?

In an attempt to protect students from harmful ultraviolet rays, recent Queensland Education Department guidelines are for school uniforms to be made of dark coloured cotton material with long sleeves. Primary schools have a policy of 'no hat, no play!' but only about 40 per cent of Grade 11 students wear hats.

**31** Does your school have an educational program relating to skin cancer? Check the information in the library for more information about this health hazard. How can you still enjoy the beach and minimise the hazard of too much sunshine?

A survey of Grade 7, 9 and 11 students by the University of Queensland's Cancer Prevention Research Centre, early in 1991, produced results along these lines:
• students are aware of the problems of skin cancer
• they think that suntans enhance appearance
• some students think that getting sunburnt occasionally does no harm
• others thought that covering up with hats, sunscreens and long sleeved shirts on the beach was not good for one's image.

**32** What do you think of the attitude of the students? What do your classmates think?
a Conduct a survey among the students in your school about their knowledge of skin cancer and their attitude towards suntans, protective clothing, the use of sunscreens, etc.
b Hold a class discussion to consider the results of your survey.

**33** Having read all the information in this chapter, do you think that Queenslander's face greater natural hazards than people in other parts of Australia?

---

**RESEARCH TOPIC 2.5**

**My local area—the natural environment**
In many areas all traces of the natural environment have been destroyed and you will have to depend on historical reports, or a book on local history, for information to be able to complete this assignment. Use sketch maps, diagrams and graphs where possible.
a Draw a map to define your local area. Is it a city, a suburb, a shire?

b What major landform features are there in the area?
c Draw a climatic graph to show the temperature/rainfall of the area. Explain the factors which influence the climate.
d What are the main features of the natural vegetation? Are there any examples of the natural vegetation left in the area?
e Do you have any natural hazards in the area? What are they?

---

**End notes**
1 *Biodiversity*, Queensland National Parks and Wildlife Service pamphlet BP522-1, November 1990, page 2
2 *Biodiversity*, page 1
3 David Attenborough, 'World Heritage values of Australia's Wet Tropical Forests', Australian Conservation Foundation Information Sheet, 1 June 1987
4 'Patterns of treated non-melanoma skin cancer in Queensland', *The Medical Journal of Australia*, Vol.153, No.5, 1990

# Chapter 3

# THE PEOPLE OF QUEENSLAND

Figure 3.1 Which ones are the Queenslanders?

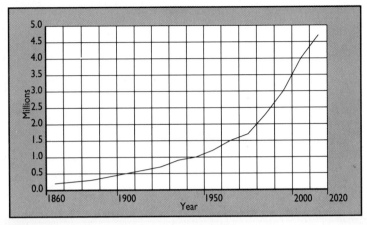

Figure 3.2 Population growth, Queensland 1860–2010

Who is a Queenslander? Is a Queenslander someone who was born there? Someone who lives there? Are Queenslanders different to people in other states? Can you identify the Queenslanders in the photograph, Figure 3.1?

## Population growth

For the past two decades Queensland has been Australia's fastest growing state, attracting settlers from both overseas countries as well as other Australian states.

1  Look at the line graph, Figure 3.2.
a  In what year did the population first exceed one million people?
b  How long did it take for the population to double?
c  If the present rate of growth continues, about how many years from 1990 will it take for the population to double again?
d  What is the estimated population for the year 2021?

## The original settlers

Long before the arrival of European settlers two groups of indigenous people had settled in that part of Australia which is now the state of Queensland—Aborigines and Torres Strait Islanders.

## Aborigines

The first wave of migrants to reach Australia were the ancestors of the present day Aborigines. One theory is that they arrived by sea, about 50 000 years ago, landing on the Arnhem Land and Kimberley coasts and by 30 000 years ago settlement had spread throughout the continent. It is not known how or when the first Aborigines settled in Queensland but archaeologists, after researching two cave sites in north Queensland, have indicated an occupancy time of at least 18 000 years.

The Aborigines lived through-out Queensland, in various areas associated with tribal units. The tribal units were small because, being subsistence hunters and food gatherers, they were linked to the carrying capacity of the land. Cultural ties to plants, animals and the landscape evolved over count-less generations. Land management, the use of fire, hunting and food gathering, movement from place to place, and environmental relation-ships were inter woven. Although there were similarities in culture there were also marked differences. Coastal Aborigines had both rainforest and coastal environments

which provided a wide variety of food, but tribal units in the drier regions to the west had to survive in a much harsher environment with a much lower land carrying capacity.

What was the impact of European settlement on the Aboriginal population? In 1859, when Queensland became a separate colony, the Aboriginal population was estimated at between ten and fifteen thousand people. The original numbers were rapidly decimated by disease, alcoholism, killings and loss of tribal land which followed the frontier of European settlement in Queensland.

Many Aborigines were taken from their tribal land and re-settled in far away places. Cherbourg, west of Gympie, and Palm Island, off the coast near Townsville, are two examples. In 1906 Cherbourg was reserved as an Aboriginal settlement and people, representing many tribes from various parts of Queensland, were forced to walk from their homelands to the site, where they were placed under the control of the Protector of Aborigines. They included members of the Culidy tribe from the Roma–Quilpie area and the Waka Waka from the Dalby–Maidenwell area. Others came from Cape York, and central western Queensland. In 1986 the settlement became independent and now runs its own community through the Cherbourg Community Council.

Aboriginal people were not included in official census counts until 1971. During the period 1971 to 1986 the Aboriginal population increased from 24 414 to 48 098 people. One reason for the increase is that census figures gave a more accurate picture of the Aboriginal population. Also, many people are now proud to identify with their Aboriginal culture and record this on census forms. In 1978 the Commonwealth government accepted a 'working definition' of Aboriginality as 'An Aborigine or Torres Strait Islander is a person of Aboriginal or Thursday Islander descent who identifies as an Aborigine or Torres Strait Islander and is accepted as such by the community with which he/she is associated'. Therefore, the definition is one of self perception. It was 1962 before all Aborigines had the right to enrol and vote in federal elections and subsequently the right to claim social security benefits. However, Aborigines still suffer from many disadvantages, including unemployment, poor housing, poverty and low economic, legal and social status.

---

**2** Read the articles in Figures 3.3 and 3.4. Discuss the issues raised in the articles. What are your opinions on the various issues?

---

**3** Where do Aborigines live in Queensland? Photocopy Map C on page 90. Look at Table 3.1.

a Show distribution of the Aboriginal population by using pie graphs, proportional circles, shading or another method. Include a legend and title on the map.

b Describe the distribution of Aborigines.

---

**Table 3.1 Aboriginal and Torres Strait Islander population, Queensland 1986**

| Statistical division | Aborigines | % total Aborigines | Torres Strait Islanders | % total Torres Strait Islanders |
|---|---|---|---|---|
| Brisbane | 9 956 | 20.3 | 1 322 | 10.0 |
| Moreton | 1 918 | 4.0 | 315 | 2.4 |
| Wide Bay/Burnett | 3 000 | 6.2 | 214 | 1.6 |
| Darling Downs | 1 806 | 3.8 | 111 | 0.8 |
| South-west | 1 831 | 3.8 | 27 | 0.2 |
| Fitzroy | 4 081 | 8.5 | 479 | 3.6 |
| Central West | 611 | 1.3 | 16 | 0.1 |
| Mackay | 1 161 | 2.4 | 1 060 | 8.0 |
| Northern | 5 506 | 11.5 | 1 669 | 12.9 |
| Far North | 11 456 | 23.8 | 7 669 | 58.2 |
| North-west | 6 772 | 14.1 | 240 | 1.8 |
| | **48 098** | | **13 122** | |

The largest concentrations of Aborigines and Torres Strait Islanders are at

- Townsville—3 123
- Torres Strait Islands—1 858
- Mt Isa—2 289
- Palm Island—1 536
- Cherbourg—944
- Toowoomba—1 020
- Rockhampton—1 645
- Cairns—2 949
- Yarrabah—1 424

---

# Blacks ask for wide power on communities

### by TONY KOCH

Aborigines and Islanders have asked the Queensland Government to introduce legislation giving them total control over their lives, including law and order, justice, education, health and employment.

They want the Queensland Parliament to acknowledge that the rights of indigenous people were eroded by colonisation and racism.

The recommendations are contained in a report given yesterday to the Deputy Premier, Mr Burns, and the Aboriginal Affairs Minister, Ms Warner.

The document was compiled by the five Aboriginal and Islander members of the legislation review committee who were asked by the Government to inquire into the legislation relating to the management of communities.

Mr Burns yesterday said the Government would now study the 87 recommendations and consider the question of funding.

The report says that as access to adequate funding and control over the use of funds is fundamental to the success of Aboriginal and Torres Strait Islander community government, three to five year funding agreements must be reached with the federal and state governments.

A major recommendation which sets out the scope of the self-government the people want says: "Each Aboriginal and Torres Strait Islander community government structure should have powers and functions over local government matters including the Building, Health, Water, Sewerage and Water Supply and Noise Abatement Acts."

Power and functions should also include:

- Education of its community members.
- Housing, social and welfare services.
- Health services.
- Employment and training.
- Operation of business, professions and trades.
- Recognition of customary rights, laws and traditions not inconsistent with rights, functions, powers, responsibilities of landowners.
- Administration of justice, policing and correctional services.
- Maintenance of peace, order and safety.
- Conservation and management of land, sites of significance and of natural resources.
- Prohibition of sale, barter, supply, manufacture or possession of alcohol, drugs and other substances of abuse.
- The conduct of community elections and referendums.
- Power to make community laws.

Figure 3.3 (The *Courier-Mail*, 27 November 1991)

# A question of land rights

The long-standing alliance between conservation and Aboriginal rights groups is falling apart.
**GREG ROBERTS** reports from Queensland, where moves to allow Aboriginals to claim ownership of national parks have created division.

Australia's best-known poet, Mrs Judith Wright-McKinney, last week made one of the most difficult decisions of her distinguished life. She resigned as patron of one of the country's largest and oldest conservation groups, the Wildlife Preservation Society of Queensland (WPSQ). Mrs Wright-McKinney has turned her back on the organisation she has worked tirelessly for since she helped form it 29 years ago.

In an open letter to the WPSQ's 1600 members to be published soon, Mrs Wright-McKinney condemns the society for being one of the chief opponents of Aboriginal land rights in Queensland. "I must disassociate myself completely from an organisation opposed to land rights and therefore have no option but to resign the patronship," she wrote.

Her move highlights how the long-standing alliance between the conservation and Aboriginal rights movements is at risk of disintegrating. In Queensland, environmentalists are bitterly divided over the Goss Government's recently introduced land rights legislation because it allows Aborigines to claim ownership of national parks. The row threatens to spread nationally, with the Australian Conservation Foundation under fire from some members over its pro-land rights stance.

The WPSQ and some other conservation groups, particularly in North Queensland, have adopted policies strongly opposing Aboriginal control of national parks and a legislative provision allowing Aborigines to hunt within their borders. Other groups, including the ACF and the Queensland Conservation Council, say parks can and should be properly managed and protected under Aboriginal ownership.

When the land rights bill is proclaimed later this month, 4.6 million hectares of national park, or 2.7 per cent of the state, will be claimable by the Aborigines. Parks that are certain to be claimed include the resort islands of Green and Fitzroy, near Cairns, Iron Range, Archer River Bend, and the major tourist attractions of Mossman Gorge and Fraser Island. The Kuku Yalanji tribe has said it will apply to hunt cassowaries and other wildlife in the Mossman Gorge and Daintree national parks.

Some conservationists say it is inconceivable that Aborigines should be permitted to hunt rare wildlife with modern firearms in the relatively small proportion of land protected as national park. Mrs Wright-McKinney disagrees. While declining to comment on her resignation as WPSQ patron, she referred to Kakadu and other Northern Territory parks that are owned by Aborigines. "If it hadn't been for the Aborigines' systems of management, their respect for the country, their self-control, we would never have had these areas to take over in the first place. They are a darned sight better at managing than we are."

The acrimony that the issue is generating within the conservation movement is probably unprecedented. Normally staid members of the WPSQ's state executive trade insults as they struggle unsuccessfully at meeting after meeting to reach a consensus. Mrs Sylvia Monk resigned after 25 years as a devoted WPSQ member. She cut the society out of her will — it had been left 10 per cent of her estate — and demanded the return of an interest-free loan. Mrs Monk said that by coming out in opposition to land rights, the society had consciously sacrificed Mrs Wright-McKinney, whose position was well-known. She said this was done to pacify some of the WPSQ's regional branches, which had threatened to disaffiliate. "The whole thing is dreadful and it's been orchestrated from parts of Queensland where people have been steeped in hatred of Aboriginal people for generations."

Aboriginal groups are angered and perplexed by the anti-land rights stand adopted by some of their former allies. To try to heal the rift, the Queensland Aboriginal Coordinating Council last week staged a three-day conference, Working Together For Our Future, at Yarrabah, near Cairns.

The conference organiser, Ms Barbara Miller, said the view that white Australians could manage national parks better than Aborigines was racist. She said the issue threatened to end 20 years of close liaison between Aboriginal and conservation groups, which had been united in their opposition to activities ranging from rainforest clearing to the Cape York space-port. Ms Miller said she believed the Government had deliberately tried to drive a wedge between the two movements.

Under the presidency of rock singer Peter Garrett and the directorship of the former Central Land Council lawyer Phillip Toyne, the Australian Conservation Foundation, Australia's biggest conservation group, has become increasingly vocal in its support for land rights.

That stand is now being challenged by some members. In a letter to Mr Garrett, ACF member Mr Harry Dick, of Cooktown, referred to the "treachery" of the ACF and other groups in supporting the Queensland land right to hunt in national parks and it is just not on with Aborigines."

The ACF's biodiversity coordinator, Mr Michael Krockenberger, says he is puzzled by the Queensland protests because in the Northern Territory, conservationists had "overwhelmingly" endorsed Aboriginal ownership of national parks. Mr Krockenberger said concerns about hunting would be adequately addressed in the management plans which, under the Queensland law, must be prepared for any park over which Aboriginal title is granted. He said that while the issue had the potential to split the green movement in Queensland, he did not believe it would do so nationally.

Support for the anti-land rights push is strong within the ranks of the Queensland Public Service. In an internal memorandum, the North Queensland director of the National Parks and Wildlife Service, Mr Bill Fisher, said the Government rushed into formulating a land rights policy with an "apparent void of informed consideration", while changing the protective status of national parks had "very serious potential to weaken the status for all time".

The president of the Cairns WPSQ branch, Ms Jill Thorsborne, has been leading the push to force the Government to exempt national parks from land claims. In a letter to the ABC's 'Four Corners' program, Ms Thorsborne said the Government had manipulated sympathetic individuals in the conservation movement to support its legislation. She said that in exchange for a Labour Party pre-election promise to double the state's area of national park, these conservationists had agreed not to publicly criticise the land rights move.

In recent months, the North Queensland press has published stories predicting the widespread extinction of wildlife if Aborigines gain control of national parks. Critics claim that under the legislation, Aborigines will be able to use guns, off-road vehicles, and power boats to hunt and fish in parks. They predict the looming destruction will be more severe than any amount of forest logging in the past.

Mrs Wright-McKinney argues it is legally doubtful that Aborigines were ever actually banned from hunting in national parks. In any event, there is no evidence suggesting that they are now planning an all-out assault on park wildlife.

The Government says there are sufficiently stringent conditions under its legislation to protect national parks. To claim a park, Aborigines have to prove the land had high value for them and demonstrate a need for ownership. An assessment of the impact of Aboriginal use on the park must be made. Parks over which a successful claim is made are to be managed jointly by Aborigines and the Government, and be leased back to the Crown for a peppercorn rent.

Aboriginal groups say that if national parks are exempted, there would be very little left under the legislation to claim, other than 3.1 million hectares in Queensland already under some secure form of Aboriginal tenure. The Government's eagerness to pacify the mining, pastoral and other interest groups had ensured that about 94 per cent of the state is out of bounds to Aboriginal claims.

Figure 3.4 (The *Age*, 12 November 1991)

## Torres Strait Islanders

The Torres Strait Islands are an Australian possession administered as part of the state of Queensland. The location of the international border was decided in 1978 after negotiations between Papua New Guinea and Australian officials. The people have special status under the *Aborigines' and Torres Strait Islanders' Affairs Act* of 1965. They have a vote in both federal and state elections and are eligible for Commonwealth social service pensions and other benefits.

---

**4** Papua New Guinea and Queensland.

a Where is the political boundary between Australia and Papua New Guinea located?

b Can you think of any problems the location of this boundary may cause?

c How far is Papua New Guinea from Cape York?

---

The Torres Strait Islands, until about ten thousand years ago, were part of a land bridge linking the Australian mainland and Papua New Guinea. Early reports by explorers indicate that the people, using fleets of large canoes, travelled from island to island and visited the mainland of New Guinea. As a result, the influence of both Melanesian and Polynesian cultures is evident, with the people of the eastern group of islands being generally of Polynesian descent and those of the western islands being Melanesian.

There is also evidence of the intermingling of the European, Japanese, Chinese and Malay peoples who were attracted to the islands from the 1870s onwards. These peoples visited the islands to work in the pearl shell, beche-de-mer and trochus shell industries.

**5** Torres Strait Islanders and Queensland.

a What was the approximate population of Torres Strait Islanders in 1986?

b Where do most Torres Strait islanders live? Construct a simple distribution map similar to the one for Aborigines and using the same map. (Far North also includes the 4837 Torres Strait Islanders who live on the islands.)

c Describe the distribution of Torres Strait Islanders. Is it similar to that of the Aborigines?

## The first European settlers

The first European settlement took place in Queensland in 1824 when a penal settlement was established near the present site of Brisbane. By the 1840s the first squatters had moved into the grazing lands of the present Darling Downs region. Until 1859 Queensland was part of the colony of New South Wales, but in that year became a separate colony with a population of 23 520 people.

As the colony was opened up by explorers and squatters, further waves of free settlers arrived from the southern colonies to be followed later by shiploads of migrant settlers from England. For the first one hundred years the great majority of overseas migrants were to be from a European background.

From the mid-1850s gold rushes, like those experienced in New South Wales and Victoria, brought thousands of people to the young state. The first rush in 1858 at Canoona (near present day Rockhampton) attracted between 15 000 and 20 000 prospectors. Gold discoveries at Gympie in 1867 saw the population of that settlement swell to 25 000 people. Just eight years after the discovery of

gold in 1871, Charters Towers became the second largest settlement in the state, with a population of 26 215. Three years after the Palmer River gold discoveries in 1872, over 40 000 people were on the goldfields. The last major gold discovery of the nineteenth century, at Croydon in 1886, attracted 7000 miners. (These places are located on the map, Figure 5.2.)

The discovery of gold in Queensland led to both an increase in population and settlement and a dramatic increase in state revenue. This growth encouraged the development of infrastructure such as roads, railways and ports which, in turn, opened the way for further settlement as pastoral, agricultural, mining and other activities were further developed.

## The first Asian migrants

The discovery of gold was also the beginning of non-European migration to Queensland as thousands of Chinese were attracted to the goldfields. There were more than 10 000 Chinese miners on the Palmer River field: most had arrived by ship and travelled overland to the goldfields from the port of Cooktown.

Chinese communities were always to be found on the Australian goldfields and it was on the goldfields that hostility towards Chinese people developed. This hostility led to punitive campaigns being undertaken by groups of miners. Chinese were entering Queensland and making their way overland to other states so in 1887 the Queensland colonial government introduced a poll tax of

10 pounds on every Chinese in order to discourage their entry. Later, bans were placed on Chinese migrants entering other states. With federation in 1901 the state bans eventually developed into the 'White Australia' policy (the *Immigration Restriction Act*, 1901) which restricted the entry into Australia of Asian and Pacific Islanders. This Act was to remain until the 1960s, when a general change in the attitude of Australians to Asian immigration resulted in its repeal.

## The arrival of Pacific Islanders

The first group of Pacific Islanders were brought to Australia in the early 1860s to work on cotton and sugar cane plantations, located in the Brisbane area. The Pacific Islanders were referred to as Kanakas, from a Polynesian word meaning 'man'. The Queensland cotton industry declined but with the spread of sugar cane plantations along the east coast the demand for indentured Pacific Islander labour continued. The islanders were to work for a period of three years and then be returned to their homes. Although many islanders volunteered and signed contracts, some people who recruited islanders were ruthless and many of the people were kidnapped. The term used for this trade in people was 'blackbirding'. Between 1863 and 1904 over 60 000 Pacific Islanders were recruited and transported to Queensland. Although there was opposition to this cruel practice the laws of the colony were powerless to control the trade and by 1891 over 9000

Kanakas were under contract. Later, because of growing opposition to this practice, the government put a ban on 'blackbirding' and offered growers a bounty to cover the extra cost of labour. Between 1904 and 1906, 3600 Kanakas who had been in Australia for less than twenty years were repatriated but others were allowed to remain in Queensland.

---

**6** Where did the Pacific Islanders come from? Use Figure 3.5.

a From which island group were most Pacific Islanders recruited?

b How far are these various island groups from Brisbane?

c Islanders were recruited from the different island groups at various times between the 1860s and 1890s. Can you suggest some reasons for this?

---

## Queensland's multicultural heritage

The arrival of migrant settlers to Queensland played a significant part in its historical/social development during the first hundred years of statehood. Does this settlement pattern of the past continue today? Are today's Queenslanders Queensland born or migrant settlers? For the past two decades Queensland has been Australia's fastest growing state, with an annual population growth rate of about 2.5 per cent.

The components of population change are natural increase (that is, people born in the country) or through migration (the arrival of people from either other states or overseas countries).

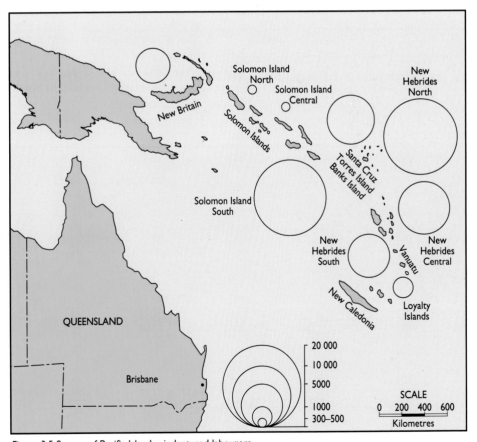

Figure 3.5 Source of Pacific Islander indentured labourers

**7** Use Figure 3.6.

a Describe the patterns of natural increase in population shown on the graph.

b What was the approximate natural increase in population in Queensland in 1989–90?

c Where did all the other people come from?

## Recent patterns of migration to Queensland

Traditionally, overseas migrants to Queensland have been of European origin. Cultural and economic links with Europe were very strong and in the years following the Second World War millions of people from the war-ravaged European countries arrived in Australia. However, in more recent years there has been a shift away from the traditional European source and people from many non-European nations are now accepted as migrants. During the past ten years Queensland's share of the total net overseas migration to Australia has varied between 11 and 14 per cent.

**8** Use Figure 3.6.

a Describe the patterns of overseas migration shown on the graph.

b How many people arrived in Queensland from overseas in 1989–90?

c Suggest reasons for the great variations shown on the graph.

d Table 3.2 shows the country of birth for major population groups in Queensland in 1966 and 1986. What do you consider to be significant changes in the source of overseas migrants to Queensland over this period of time?

e The statistics show Australia as the birthplace for a large number of people. What other information would you need from this group to get an accurate picture of the extent of Queensland's multi-racial background?

**9** Use Tables 3.3 and 3.4.

a What changes have taken place in the pattern of Asian migration to Queensland since 1981?

b What is the pattern of Pacific Islander migration to Queensland in the period shown?

c Can you suggest some reasons for the change?

d Many Pacific Islanders prefer to settle in Queensland rather than in other states. Suggest some reasons.

### Table 3.2 Queensland, major population groups 1966–86

| Birthplace | 1966 | 1986 |
|---|---|---|
| Australia | 1 480 832 | 2 162 995 |
| New Zealand | 7 608 | 61 246 |
| UK/Eire | 106 112 | 1 158 949 |
| Netherlands | 9 868 | 14 272 |
| Germany | 9 026 | 15 780 |
| Italy | 20 272 | 17 418 |
| Other Europe | 29 027 | 43 472 |
| Asia | 9 330 | 37 917 |
| Other | 10 613 | 75 266 |
| **Total** | **1 682 688** | **3 587 315** |

### Table 3.3 Major source of Asian settlers

| Birthplace | 1981 | 1986 |
|---|---|---|
| China | 2 773 | 3 536 |
| Hong Kong | 1 166 | 2 332 |
| India | 2 938 | 3 573 |
| Indonesia | 2 101 | 2 562 |
| Japan | 575 | 1 230 |
| Malaysia | 2 955 | 4 317 |
| Philippines | 1 405 | 4 519 |
| Singapore | 1 147 | 1 818 |
| Sri Lanka | 1 260 | 1 747 |
| Vietnam | 3 508 | 6 234 |

### Table 3.4 Major source of Pacific Islanders

| Birthplace | 1981 | 1986 |
|---|---|---|
| Cook Islands | 67 | 207 |
| Fiji | 1 367 | 2 369 |
| New Caledonia | 132 | 256 |
| New Zealand | 48 018 | 61 246 |
| Papua New Guinea | 7 876 | 9 785 |
| Solomon Islands | 175 | 260 |
| Tonga | 269 | 438 |
| Western Samoa | 134 | 655 |

The number and origin of migrants to Australia is determined by the Commonwealth government's migration policy program. Over the past forty-five years migrant quotas have averaged between 100 000 and 140 000 people a year. The quota for the year 1990–91 was set at 126 000 people. Migrant quotas are at present based on various eligibility categories. For example, in the first part of 1991, 44 per cent of settlers arrived in Australia under the family

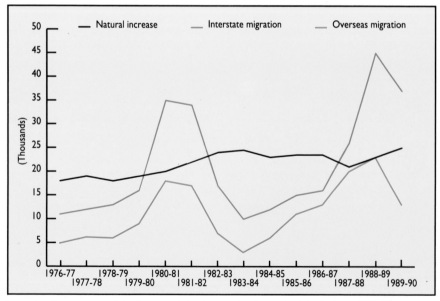

Figure 3.6 Components of absolute population increase in Queensland, 1976–77 to 1989–90

reunion component, 40 per cent under the skilled component, and 6 per cent under the humanitarian component. Other categories include refugee and special admission.

**10** Discuss the following questions as a class.

a Why does the federal government change the migrant quotas and categories from time to time?

b Do you think we should have more or less migrants?

c Where do you think our migrant settlers should come from?

d How would you decide who is eligible to enter Australia?

e Where would many settlers, who are currently arriving under the humanitarian or refugee component, originate?

f Some people arrive in Australia illegally. Should they be given priority above those people who have been waiting years to be accepted? What are your views on this?

On being accepted into Australia migrants are generally free to settle in any part of the country—many choose Queensland. In 1986 15 per cent of Queensland's population was migrant settlers. New South Wales and Victoria have always attracted the greater share of overseas settlers, following a traditional pattern. About 63 per cent of Australia's overseas born population live in those two states.

**11** Use Table 3.5.

a Which migrant groups tend to favour settling in Queensland?

b Most migrants settle in large cities. Does Brisbane attract a higher percentage of migrants than other Queensland urban areas? Suggest reasons for this.

**Table 3.5 Major birthplace groups and their representation in Queensland compared to all Australia and Brisbane compared to all Queensland**

| | Number 1986 | Percentage of national total | Percentage in Brisbane |
|---|---|---|---|
| Australia | 2 162 995 | 17.9* | 42.5** |
| UK/Eire | 158 949 | 14.1 | 55.9 |
| Italy | 17 418 | 6.7 | 46.4 |
| Germany | 15 780 | 13.7 | 47.6 |
| Greece | 4 048 | 2.9 | 74.5 |
| Netherlands | 14 272 | 15.0 | 51.9 |
| Yugoslavia | 7 544 | 5.0 | 63.2 |
| New Zealand | 61 246 | 28.9* | 48.3 |
| Poland | 4 843 | 7.2 | 69.1 |
| Vietnam | 6 234 | 7.5 | 92.4 |
| USSR | 2 666 | 7.6 | 68.0 |
| Malaysia | 4 317 | 9.0 | 67.2 |
| USA | 7 395 | 17.4* | 44.2** |
| India | 3 573 | 7.5 | 67.7 |
| Hungary | 2 330 | 8.6 | 52.1 |
| Malta | 2 536 | 4.5 | 38.4** |
| Austria | 2 260 | 10.0 | 43.3** |
| Latvia | 886 | 8.2 | 60.6 |
| Cyprus | 1 229 | 5.2 | 70.5 |
| South Africa | 4 996 | 13.5 | 61.5 |
| China | 3 536 | 9.4 | 69.1 |
| Czechoslovakia | 1 696 | 9.5 | 47.0 |
| Canada | 3 962 | 19.4* | 45.2 |
| Philippines | 4 519 | 13.4 | 46.3 |
| Lebanon | 791 | 1.4 | 74.2 |
| France | 2 319 | 15.6 | 55.8 |
| Egypt | 1 001 | 3.3 | 58.3 |
| Papua New Guinea | 9 785 | 45.8* | 55.4 |
| Singapore | 1 818 | 11.1 | 61.1 |
| Spain | 2 019 | 12.4 | 63.2 |
| Hong Kong | 2 332 | 8.2 | 67.4 |
| Sri Lanka | 1 747 | 7.8 | 79.3 |
| Indonesia | 2 562 | 14.5 | 62.3 |
| Turkey | 352 | 1.4 | 49.4 |
| Chile | 706 | 3.8 | 86.5 |
| Portugal | 530 | 3.6 | 84.5 |

\* Above overall Queensland percentage of national population (16.6 per cent)
\*\*Below average proportion of state population in Brisbane Statistical Division (44.4 per cent)

**12** You and your family are migrating to a foreign country. Your father can speak only a few words of the language, other family members only speak your own national language. You have arrived in a large city of the country in which you plan to settle and have been transferred to a migrant centre. You do not have much money. List the things that would be important in determining where you will settle in your new country. Place them in a priority order.

Now hold a class discussion to consider this situation. Some members may be able to contribute from personal experience. How similar or different are their reasons to the ones that you listed?

## Settlers from interstate

During the past two decades more than one-third of the population increase in Queensland was gained from interstate migration. But this is a two-way flow as many people have also left Queensland to live in other states.

**13** Use Figures 3.6 and 3.7.

a  Between 1981 and 1986 Queensland gained 203 264 people from other Australian states, but 114 162 people left the state. What was the state's gain through net interstate migration?

b  Describe the patterns of natural increase in population shown on the graph, Figure 3.6.

c  Where did the people come from? Look at the flow chart, Figure 3.7, to answer this question.

d  Describe the pattern of migration in to and out of Queensland.

## Why do people migrate?

The reasons why people leave one country or place to settle in another can be referred to as 'push–pull' factors. Push factors are those which tend to make people want to leave their home country or state. Examples of push factors are war, unemployment, political dissent, poverty. Pull factors are those which attract people to a new place or country. Examples are employment opportunities, availability of land, lifestyle, religious/political tolerance, relatives already established.

**14** Think about migration.

a  Name some other push and pull factors.

b  Why do you think that people migrated to Queensland last century? List some of the pull factors that attracted early migrants to Queensland.

c  List some of the push factors that you think may have been a reason for them to leave their former home.

d  Suggest some reasons why people from other states migrate to Queensland today.

**15** Use Table 3.5.

a  On a map of the world shade the countries from which people migrated to Queensland. Use the statistics in Table 3.5 but for convenience do not include UK/Eire because of the great numbers compared to other settlers. Here is a suggested scale or you may like to calculate your own: < 999; 1000–1999; 2000–2999 etc. Choose your own shading pattern. Complete the map with a title and key.

b  Find out more about the countries through the media. Mark with an * those countries where current political/economic problems may cause people to want to migrate.

c  What conditions in the particular countries may have acted as push factors? Remember that the figures are for 1986.

d  What factors may encourage people from the more recent migrant groups to leave their homeland?

**16** Do you think that recent events in Eastern Europe will encourage people to migrate to Australia? What could prevent them from doing so? Discuss.

**17** Conduct a class survey on migration. This survey could also be extended to survey all students in the school. Use the statistics to draw distribution maps or graphs and discuss the pattern shown. Your local or school library may have statistics from the Australian Bureau of Statistics. See if they have the statistics for your local area and if so, draw a graph to show the ethnic composition of the area. Do you live in a multicultural neighbourhood?

a  How many people in your class were born in Australia?

b  For those not born in Australia, where were they born?

c  Where were their parents born?

**18** Is the population of Queensland evenly distributed across the state? Look at Table 3.6.

a  Photocopy Map C on page 90 and use it to show the population distribution. Decide the best way to show this information.

b  Describe the distribution of population.

c  Which statistical divisions have the greatest proportion of the total population?

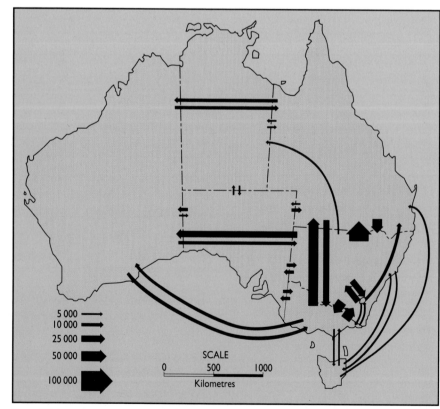

5 000
10 000
25 000
50 000
100 000

SCALE
0    500    1000
Kilometres

Figure 3.7 Australia, interstate migration flows, 1981–86

| Table 3.6 Queensland's population, 1991 and 2006 | | |
|---|---|---|
| Statistical division | Population 1991 | Estimated population 2006 |
| Brisbane | 1 325 402 | 1 673 962 |
| Moreton | 528 760 | 828 012 |
| Darling Downs | 191 769 | 224 402 |
| Wide Bay-Burnett | 190 715 | 239 796 |
| Far North | 189 543 | 258 869 |
| Northern | 183 428 | 230 597 |
| Fitzroy | 168 074 | 206 118 |
| Mackay | 112 242 | 145 253 |
| North-west | 38 725 | 39 527 |
| South-west | 28 783 | 29 785 |
| Central West | 13 292 | 13 084 |

d   Which statistical division will have the greatest growth rate by the year 2006? Suggest some reasons for the growth.

## Where do Queenslanders work?

The number of people who are available for employment are referred to as the workforce.

**19** Answer these questions.

a   Use Table 3.7 to determine how many people were in the Queensland workforce in 1991.

b   What percentage of the total Queensland population are in the workforce?

c   For statistical purposes, broad categories of employment type are used. Which types of work employ the most people?

d   Much of Queensland's GSP comes from the primary industries. What percentage of people are employed in these activities?

e   Look at the composition of manufacturing turnover shown in Figure 3.8. Which are the two most important industries? Can you suggest some reasons why?

f   What percentage of the workforce is located in Brisbane?

g   Suggest reasons why Brisbane offers greater employment opportunities than other parts of the state. Is this also true for other Australian capital cities?

h   The percentage of people in the workforce who are unable to obtain employment varies from time to time according to the economic situation. When the most recent unemployment figures are released find out whether the percentage of unemployed in Queensland is higher or lower than for the rest of Australia. Find out the number of people concerned. Are there any specific age groups or occupations most disadvantaged?

## Age structure of Queensland's population

Does Queensland have a youthful population, an old population? Is it important? Demography is the scientific study of human populations. Demographers are particularly interested in three broad age groups
* the number of people aged 0–15 (child dependency group)
* the number aged 16–64 ( the working ages)
* the number aged 65+ (the aged dependency group).

From statistics for these three groups demographers calculate the 'dependency ratio'—the number of people aged 0 to 15 and those over 65 per 100 persons of working age. For example, in 1987 for every 100 persons in employment, 51.7 people

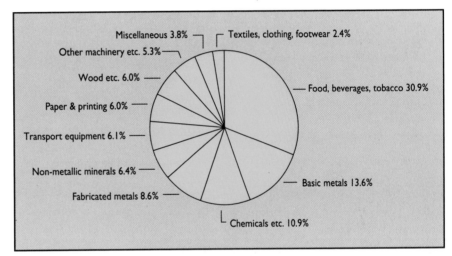

Figure 3.8 Composition of manufacturing turnover, 1988–89

| Table 3.7 Employment, Queensland and Brisbane, November 1991 | | | | |
|---|---|---|---|---|
| Employment | Number Qld | % of total Qld | Number Brisbane | Brisbane's share % |
| Agriculture, forestry fishing, hunting | 90 100 | 6.8 | 7 000 | 0.8 |
| Mining | 21 300 | 1.6 | 2 300 | 10.8 |
| Manufacturing | 152 700 | 11.5 | 82 400 | 54.0 |
| Electricity, gas, water | 13 100 | 1.0 | 7 200 | 55.0 |
| Construction | 111 500 | 8.4 | 49 200 | 44.1 |
| Wholesale/retail trade | 294 000 | 22.2 | 148 000 | 50.3 |
| Transport/storage | 74 300 | 5.6 | 37 200 | 50.0 |
| Communication | 21 100 | 1.6 | 11 400 | 54.0 |
| Finance, property, business services | 129 300 | 9.8 | 76 800 | 59.4 |
| Public admin. defence | 51 300 | 3.9 | 28 800 | 56.1 |
| Community services | 248 700 | 18.8 | 122 900 | 49.4 |
| Recreation, personal and other services | 116 400 | 8.8 | 41 400 | 35.6 |
| **Total** | **1 323800** | **100** | **614 600** | **46.4** |

were dependent on them. The labour force produces the goods and services required to sustain society's non-working population.

**20** Conduct a class discussion using the following questions.

a   What are the special needs of the child dependency group? Consider the things that are provided for you by those other than your parents.

b   What are the special needs of the aged dependency group? Perhaps you could use your grandparents as a resource for this?

c   In what ways are these two groups dependent on the working ages group?

d   Can you think of some groups of people in the 15 to 64 age groups who are also dependent on the working population?

e   More people are becoming dependent on fewer workers. What are the implications of this for Queensland?

## Age-structure pyramids

One way of graphically showing the age statistics of a population is by a population or age-structure pyramid. Population groups are shown as a number or a percentage of the total population.

**21** Use Figure 3.9.

a   Describe the changing pattern for Queensland's various age groups.

b   Which was the largest age group in 1986?

c   Which will be the largest age group in the year 2021?

d   What changes are apparent in the 60 plus age groups?

e   Is the population of Queensland ageing?

In June 1971 the median age for Queenslanders was 26.9 years and by June 1989 it had increased to 31.2 years. A great deal of debate and many items in the print media refer to the increasing proportion of older people in the population of Australia. In response to the ageing of the population the Queensland government established the Queensland Office of Ageing in December 1990, to develop policies and programs to meet the needs and interests of older people.

**22** The per capita costs of government programs for the elderly are generally double the per capita costs of government programs for children. Can you suggest some reasons why this is so?

**23** Look at the population facts from the Office of Ageing shown in Figure 3.10.

a   To what extent is Queensland's population ageing?

b   What percentage of Queensland's population will be aged more than 60 in the year 2011? How old will you be then?

c   In what year will you enter the 'Third Age' discussed in the extract?

d   What do you think are the special needs of the 60 plus age group?

e   Where do people of this age group live? Do they prefer some parts of Queensland more than others?

Age is both relative and subjective. You are old compared to a baby. Young children may see you as 'old' because you go to a secondary school. You see your grandparents as old. They may not consider themselves as being old. Because women are entitled to an 'old age' pension at age 60 years and men at age 65 years, these figures are generally used as the entry point to old age. If a person is over these ages he or she may be considered as old. But is this a fair measure? Some people retire from work in their 50s. Are they old? Some people continue to work until they are in their 70s. Are they old? In reality, physical ageing begins earlier than many people realise. The years between 30 and 40 see the fastest decline in the body when the ageing process is at its most vigorous!

**24** What are community attitudes to ageing? Read the extract, Figure 3.11.

a   Do you agree or disagree with the points raised?

b   Suggest some reasons why certain parts of Queensland are more favoured by the older population than others.

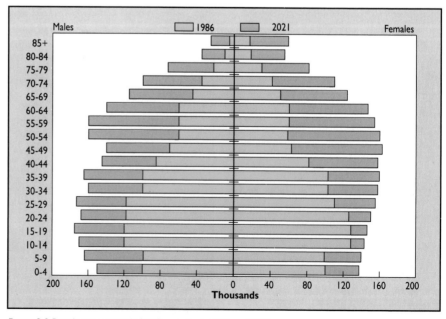

Figure 3.9 Population pyramids for Queensland, 1986 and 2021

## Population Facts

- As in most developed countries, the Australian population is ageing: that is, the proportion older than 60 years is expected to increase from 16 to 20 per cent between 1991 and 2011. For Queensland, a similar increase is expected, from 15% in 1991 to 19% in 2011.

- In the past five years, the age group over 65 years has increased at twice the rate of the total Queensland population; those over 75, two and a half times the general rate of increase.

- In the next ten years, the fastest growth is expected to occur in the older age groups: in Queensland the number of people over 75 years will increase more than twice as fast as the total population, while the projected increase over 85 years is more than three times the rate for Queensland overall.

- In less than twenty years, a further acceleration will take place as the first of the 'baby boom' generation turn 60 years.

- However, over the next twenty years, the balance between people of working age and those at younger and older ages (the "total dependency ratio") is projected to decrease.

- At all ages after 65 years, women outnumber men; by 80 years, there are twice as many women.

- The likelihood of living alone increases with age. One-fifth of people over 60, and one-quarter of those over 70 live alone. People over 60 constitute over half of Queensland's lone householders. Most older people who live alone are women.

- The Queensland areas with the highest proportion of people over 60 years are Hervey Bay 25%, Mount Morgan 24%, Gold Coast City 24%, Redcliffe 23%, Gympie 22%. Areas with low proportions of older people include Mount Isa, Logan City, Thuringowa City, and Pine Rivers Shire each 6%, and Moreton Shire 7%.

- Eighteen percent of Queensland's older population (over 60) live in areas classified as rural and remote (compared to 21% of the total population).

- In 1989 the life expectancy at birth 73 years for Queensland males and 79 years for females. One hundred years ago, the corresponding figures were 47 and 51 years.

- Of Australians in their 60's, only 7.5% are "severely handicapped." After 70 years, this increases to 24%, nearly two-thirds of whom live at home.

- The proportion of older Queenslanders born overseas is rising from 11% in 1981 to a predicted 22% in 2001. Nearly 75% of older people who speak a language other than English at home live in and around Brisbane; a further 10% live in Far North Queensland.

- The overall life expectancy for Aboriginal and Islander people is 15 to 20 years less than the average, with considerable diversity between communities. Only 5% were aged over 60 years in the 1986 census, and a further 12 % over 40 years.

Figure 3.10 Facts about ageing from the Office of Ageing

## Community Attitudes to Ageing

- A telephone survey of Queenslander's attitudes to ageing was conducted for the Office of Ageing in June 1991. A sample of 851 was selected at random from local telephone directories throughout Queensland to represent age, sex and location population distributions. Results were analysed for statistical significance.

- Although most people saw "old age" beginning at about 65 years, they tended to put a thirty-year gap between themselves and old age until they were in their mid-forties or older. "Old age" was not identified as a person's own age until they were in their seventies and in some cases later than this.

- More people could name disadvantages of being in the older age group than advantages. One-fifth of people believed there were no advantages to being older, (compared to 55 who said there were no disadvantages).

- A wide range of perceived advantages included freedom, wisdom, experience, time for activities, financial benefits, and the company of family and friends. The predominant perceived disadvantage (75% of people) was the loss of ability to do things (mostly physical); others were lack of power and respect, and loneliness/isolation.

- Younger and older people to some extent perceived older age differently. In particular, financial and health problems were regarded more seriously by younger people. People most likely to say that being older had no problems were over 70 years.

- Only about 50% of people described themselves as ageing; the proportion increased slightly after 35 years, and became much higher after the mid-fifties.

- Only about one-third of people felt positive about their own ageing; one-fifth felt concern. People most likely to be concerned, and less confident about managing their own ageing, were aged between 25 and 44 years. Those with positive attitudes to older age in general, and higher levels of contact with older people, were most likely to feel positive about their own ageing.

- Women were more likely to have a positive attitude towards older age in general. However, on a personal level they were more likely to be concerned about their own ageing, and less likely to describe themselves as ageing.

- Around one-third of people below 60 years had not made any plans for life after 70. Those who had made plans were most likely to be between the mid-forties and mid-fifties. Superannuation was the most frequently made plan, particularly by people aged between 25 and 34 years. In general, people who had made plans had a more positive attitude to older age in general and to their own ageing.

- Four terms were seen as the most acceptable descriptions of the older age group: "mature ages", "older people", "seniors", "senior citizens". "Older people" was the only term equally acceptable to all age groups. Least liked terms were : "aged people", "the aged", and "the ageing".

- Most people believed that age discrimination based on a judgement of "too old", does occur, and that it began between the forties and sixties. However only a minority believed they had experienced age discrimination, mostly in employment.

Figure 3.11 More facts about ageing from the Office of Ageing

c Over the past decade there has been a significant increase in the number of 'retirement villages' constructed. What is a retirement village? Why do you think retirement villages are popular with many older people?

d Are your grandparents retired? If so, where do they live? Did they relocate after retirement? If so, why?

25 Are Queenslanders different to other Australians? Based on the information in this chapter would you describe a typical Queenslander as a person in the 20 to 29 age group, Australian-born and living in the inner suburbs of a large urban area in the south-east of the state?

a What is wrong with such a description?

b What is your concept of a Queenslander?

**RESEARCH TOPIC 3.1**

Age and youth in my local area. From Australian Bureau of Statistics or Local Government Authority statistics, construct a population pyramid of your local area.

a Describe the population structure. Are you in an area where the population distribution is young or old?

b What provision does the local area make for the 0 to 15 age group? Discuss the programs/facilities available, map them and then describe the distribution.

c Are the needs and interests of this age group catered for in the local area?

d Now do the same research for the 60 plus age group. Is this age group catered for? Perhaps you could arrange visits to pre-school centres and retirement villages to discuss first hand the needs of each group .

Figure 3.12 It is commonly believed that older people are different—frailer, more dependent, inferior physically and mentally, and not to be envied. Do members of this senior citizens walking group fit the stereotype?

# Chapter 4

# URBAN AND RURAL ENVIRONMENTS

The movement of people between states and within states, indicates that mobility is a feature of the Australian way of life today. In Chapter 3 reference is made to the movement of people into Queensland from other states. In this chapter we will consider where Queenslanders live.

Do Queenslander's live in urban or rural areas? Is the pattern of Queensland's population distribution changing?

1 What is the pattern of movement of people within Queensland?

a Look at the flow chart, Figure 4.1. Describe the intrastate movement of people in Queensland for the period shown.

b Which regions of Queensland had an inflow of people?

c Which regions had an outflow of people?

d Does the flow chart indicate a drift from inland to coastal areas? Does it indicate a drift from rural to urban areas?

Even though Queensland is more decentralised than other Australian states it is obvious that a very high proportion of Queensland's population live in or near large urban areas.

2 Answer the following.

a How many cities in Queensland have a population of more than 20 000? Use Table 4.1 to answer this question.

b Describe the distribution of these cities. (See map, Figure 1.3.)

c Suggest some reasons why these locations may have developed as urban areas. ( Figure 4.14 and Chapter 5 have some information that should help.)

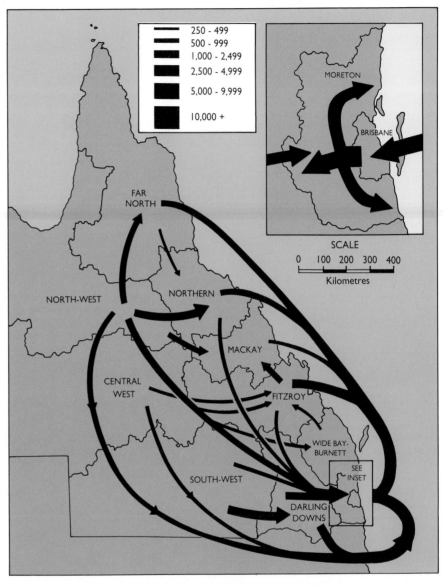

Figure 4.1 Net intrastate movement between statistical divisions, 1981-1986

| Table 4.1 Cities with a population over 20 000 | | | | | |
| Urban centre | Population 1991 | Average growth rate 1986 to 1991 % | Urban centre | Population 1991 | Average growth rate 1986 to 1991 |
|---|---|---|---|---|---|
| Brisbane City | 753 375 | 0.45 | Cairns | 44 021 | 2.02 |
| Logan City | 153 427 | 4.80 | Caloundra | 34 594 | 6.21 |
| Gold Coast City | 139 899 | 5.66 | Bundaberg | 33 470 | 0.67 |
| Townsville | 84 545 | 0.56 | Thuringowa | 31 016 | 5.20 |
| Toowoomba | 83 766 | 1.40 | Mackay | 27 700 | 0.02 |
| Ipswich | 76 673 | 0.54 | Hervey Bay City | 27 128 | 7.58 |
| Rockhampton | 59 966 | 0.88 | Mt Isa | 23 882 | -0.41 |
| Redcliffe City | 49 389 | 1.38 | Maryborough | 23 668 | 0.78 |
| | | | Gladstone | 23 289 | 0.05 |

Figure 4.2a 'Queenslanders'—a unique style of housing in both rural and urban areas of Queensland. A homestead on a north Queensland cattle property

Figure 4.2c Many country towns are physically divided by major highways and railways passing through the centre of town. To reduce traffic in Nambour, the Bruce Highway now by-passes the main street

Figure 4.2d The central business district (CBD) of Brisbane

Figure 4.2b The Grand Mariner high-rise residential building—high population density residential areas are a feature of the Gold Coast

Figure 4.2e Small country towns are losing services to nearby larger centres

Figure 4.2f Originally a town based on the timber industry, Ravenshoe was the scene of bitter conflict between loggers and environmentalists when plans to place the logging area under World Heritage protection were announced in the late 1980s

Figure 4.2g Residential areas located on a network of canals have been a feature of the development of the Gold Coast. Residential canal development has also been developed, to a lesser extent, on Moreton Bay and the Sunshine Coast. Work has started on the first residential canal estate in Cairns

Figure 4.2h The rural–urban fringe of Kingaroy. Kingaroy Shire has an average growth rate of 1.68 per cent

**Table 4.2 Ranking of LGAs according to estimated resident population, 1986 and projected population, 2001**

| LGA | Estimated resident pop 1986 | LGA | Projected population 2001 | Projected percentage growth 1986–2001 |
|---|---|---|---|---|
| Brisbane (C) | 736 656 | Brisbane (C) | 751 722 | 2.0 |
| Logan (C) | 121 337 | Albert (S) | • 246 700 | 160.5 |
| Gold Coast (C) | 120 300 | Logan (C) | 220 700 | 81.9 |
| Albert (S) | 94 685 | Gold Coast (C) | 171 729 | 42.8 |
| Townsville (C) | 82 223 | Redland (S) | 146 570 | 142.2 |
| Toowoomba (C) | 78 140 | Pine Rivers (S) | 122 362 | 59.3 |
| Pine Rivers (S) | 76 811 | Caboolture (S) | 112 143 | 130.8 |
| Ipswich (C) | 74 636 | Maroochy (S) | 105 181 | 72.3 |
| Maroochy (S) | 61 047 | Toowoomba (C) | 96 901 | 24.0 |
| Redland (S) | 60 521 | Townsville (C) | 93 707 | 14.0 |
| Rockhampton (C) | 57 384 | Moreton (S) | 92 703 | 140.9 |
| Calboolture (S) | 48 599 | Mulgrave (S) | 86 097 | 115.7 |
| Redcliffe (C) | 46 127 | Ipswich (C) | 82 522 | 10.6 |
| Mulgrave (S) | 39 907 | Thuringowa (C) | 73 047 | 139.2 |
| Cairns (C) | 39 823 | Rockhampton (C) | 72 831 | 26.9 |
| Moreton (S) | 38 487 | Caloundra (C) | 72 284 | 101.1 |
| Caloundra (C) | 35 937 | Beaudesert (S) | 56 488 | 114.1 |
| Pioneer (S) | 35 802 | Pioneer (S) | 54 222 | 51.4 |
| Bundaberg(C) | 32 368 | Cairns (C) | 50 229 | 26.1 |
| Thuringowa (C) | 30 543 | Redcliffe (C) | 50 192 | 8.8 |
| Beaudesert (S) | 26 384 | Bundaberg (C) | 36 235 | 11.9 |
| Mount Isa (C) | 24 374 | Noosa (S) | 35 692 | 90.2* |
| Gladstone (C) | 23 236 | Hervey Bay (C) | 31 533 | 67.5 |
| Maryborough (C) | 22 763 | Mount Isa (C) | 30 910 | 26.8 |
| Mackay(C) | 22 682 | Gladstone (C) | 27 384 | 17.9 |
| Hervey Bay (C) | 18 829 | Mackay (C) | 26 588 | 17.2 |
| Noosa (S) | 18 770 | Maryborough (C) | 25 601 | 12.5 |
| Burdekin (S) | 18 373 | Livingstone (S) | 23 694 | 55.0 |
| Johnstone (S) | 17 237 | Whitsunday (S) | 21 952 | 122.4 |
| Banana (S) | 16 895 | Mareeba (S) | 21 239 | 35.3 |
| Mareeba (S) | 15 698 | Johnstone (S) | 21 184 | 22.9 |
| Livingstone (S) | 15 283 | Widgee (S) | 21 125 | 53.8 |
| Bowen (S) | 13 967 | Banana (S) | 19 606 | 16.0 |
| Widgee (S) | 13 739 | Burdekin (S) | 18 782 | 2.2 |
| Hinchinbrook (S) | 13 483 | Belyando (S) | 16 548 | 44.9 |
| Gatton (S) | 12 502 | Gatton (S) | 15 996 | 27.9 |
| Woongarra (S) | 11 715 | Woongarra (S) | 15 897 | 35.7 |
| Belyando (S) | 11 424 | Douglas (S) | 15 462 | 136.2 |
| Gympie (C) | 11 263 | Calliope (S) | 15 134 | 54.8 |
| Duaringa (S) | 10 603 | Bowen (S) | 14 867 | 6.4 |
| Warwick (C) | 10 133 | Esk (S) | 13 692 | 45.8 |
| Kingaroy (S) | 10 089 | Hinchinbrook (S) | 13 337 | -1.1 |
| | | Fitzroy (S) | 13 256 | 103.4 |
| | | Duaringa (S) | 13 163 | 24.1 |
| | | Emerald (S) | 13 113 | 39.5 |
| | | Jondaryan (S) | 12 675 | 31.0 |
| | | Kingaroy (S) | 12 576 | 24.7 |
| | | Gympie (C) | 12 573 | 11.6 |
| | | Sarina (S) | 12 543 | 66.0 |
| | | Warwick (C) | 11 898 | 17.4 |
| | | Broadsound (S) | 11 464 | 33.8 |
| | | Stanthorpe (S) | 11 372 | 18.5 |
| | | Atherton (S) | 11 038 | 29.2 |
| | | Dalby (T) | 10 318 | 6.0 |
| | | Laidley (S) | 10 130 | 42.6 |

Source: ABS, *Estimated Resident Population, Queensland*, catalogue No. 3201.3. Skinner and others, 1989, *Population projections for Local Government Areas 1986-2001*, A.P.R.U.

3 Look at the photographs, Figure 4.2.

a What type of areas are shown? Rural or urban? What are the main features of each type of area?

b Where do you live? In an urban or rural area?

c Where would you prefer to live—in a rural or an urban area? Give reasons.

d Not everyone is in agreement with the type of development shown in Figure 4.2g. What are the advantages and disadvantages of development and living in such residential areas?

e Will important rural land be lost to future urban expansion?

Population projections indicate that Queensland will continue to be the fastest growing state in Australia with an estimated population of 4.7 million people by the year 2021. That is a population growth of 80 per cent between the years of 1986 and 2021, or an increase in population of 2 118 000 people!

Where will these people live? Will Queenslanders continue the trend to live in cities and large towns?

4 Look at Table 3.6.

a Describe the distribution of Queensland's population for the year 2006.

b Are existing highly populated areas continuing to grow?

c Which five statistical divisions will have the largest populations by the year 2006?

d Statistical divisions are further divided into Local Government Areas (LGAs). Which LGAs will have the highest growth rate in the year 2001? Which will have the most people? Use Table 4.2 to answer this question.

e Photocopy Map A and Map B pages 88 and 89. Make a distribution map by shading the LGAs shown on Table 4.2. Use the following scale for the shires (or you may choose to calculate your own): % population growth 0–24; 25–50; 51–75; 76–100; 101–125; 126–150; 151–175. You may choose to use column graphs to show the growth of the cities. Describe the population distribution for the year 2001 as shown on the completed map.

## South-east Queensland: Australia's future mega-city

Towards the end of this decade the twin cities of Brisbane and Gold Coast will join to form a long thin city some 150 km long. Early in the 21st century it will extend northwards to link up with the Sunshine Coast to form a continuous urban area some 250 km long. Some time around the year 2005 this elongated city will house four million people and overtake Melbourne to become the second largest urban area in Australia.[1]

The growth predicted in this report will take place in the Brisbane and Moreton statistical divisions.

5  Answer these questions about Brisbane and Moreton.

a  How many LGAs are located in the two statistical divisions?

b  Name the LGAs which may merge to form this super city.

c  Which of the three LGAs has the greatest population today?

d  Which will have the greatest population growth?

e  Which will have the greatest number of people?

f  On your copy of Map C (question 4e) draw a line around the mega-city that may develop. Suggest a name for the mega-city. Perhaps Bris-Go-Sun?

What will be the cost to the government, to society, to the environment as this mega-city develops?

The Queensland government and LGAs will have to plan for the cost of providing the growing areas with social and physical

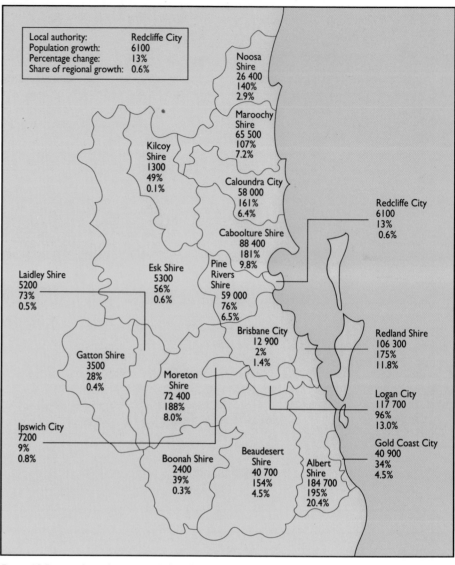

Figure 4.3 Projected population growth for LGAs in Brisbane and Moreton Statistical Divisions, 1986–2006

infrastructure such as welfare services, schools, hospitals, roads, sewerage, and water supplies. Surface water resources are adequate for the predicted population of south-east Queensland but early planning is necessary in order to acquire land for water storages. Construction of a dam is a long term project with a period of two to three years to investigate and plan the dam and a further four to six years to construct and provide all the necessary infrastructure. People want water storages but 'not in our valley!' Conflict between residents and local authorities has already taken place over proposed water storage sites.

An increase in the use of fossil fuels will be needed to meet the growing demand for power supplies and transport. People living in the newer outer suburbs could be isolated from central city services unless adequate transportation and transportation routes are provided.

As the urban areas become larger, the re-zoning of rural and other land to urban classification places added costs on the whole community. These are the costs of infrastructure—roads, water supply, power and other services that modern communities require. Sydney and Melbourne have become huge sprawling cities, taking over thousands of hectares of valuable

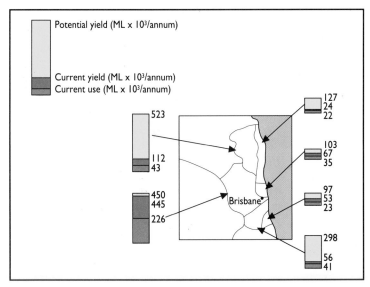

Potential yield (ML x 10³/annum)

Current yield (ML x 10³/annum)
Current use (ML x 10³/annum)

523
112
43

450
445
226

Brisbane

127
24
22

103
67
35

97
53
23

298
56
41

Figure 4.4 Surface water resources, south-east Queensland

Figure 4.5 Natural bushland is replaced by houses as residential development takes place on Brisbane's western urban fringe

cropland in the process. Can Brisbane and other Queensland urban areas learn from this?

Large areas of both the natural and rural environment will be lost as development sprawls further out from the existing urban boundaries. About 75 per cent of Brisbane's bushland is expected to be cleared if the current rate of development continues. It is estimated that the cost of developing a suburban block in outer suburban areas costs the tax payer about $40 000.

The growth in the number of households in Queensland has been greater than the growth in total population. For example between 1981 and 1990 the number of dwellings increased by 34.4 per cent while the population grew at a rate of 23.9 per cent. In general terms every 100 000 people will require 36 000 new dwellings, an average of 21 600 new dwellings per year between 1986 and 2021!

With the decrease in areas of natural bushland wildlife habitats are also threatened unless wildlife corridors are established. South-east Queensland has significant areas of koala habitat which need to be protected.

## Brisbane: Planning for the twenty-first century

Although Brisbane city has a lower percentage growth rate than neighbouring areas it is still expected to have a population of about 750 000 in the year 2001. The current trend for Brisbane's population growth is to slow, as younger families are forced to move to outer suburbs and neighbouring LGAs where houses and land are less expensive. Unless present patterns of residential development are changed and the community accepts the concept of high density housing, the main residents of Brisbane will be the old and the more affluent.

6  Suggest some reasons for the change in household size. What are the implications for residential areas and houses if households become smaller? What changes do you see for the future?

7  Answer these questions.
a  What are the present patterns of residential development in urban areas? How should these change in order to meet the demands of future residents? How can this change be achieved?
b  What is the 'Green Street' concept of residential development?
c  Both federal and state governments advocate a change in our patterns of residential development through the 'Better Cities' program. What is this program?
d  What are 'gentrification' and 'traffic calming'? What changes do they make in inner suburbs? What changes can

| Table 4.3 Household growth by size of household and percentage distribution Queensland, 1986–2006 | | | | | | |
|---|---|---|---|---|---|---|
| Household size | 1986 | | 1996* | | 2006* | |
| persons per dwelling | Number | % | Number | % | Number | % |
| 1 person | 152 303 | 18.27 | 244 633 | 21.58 | 346 652 | 24.20 |
| 2 persons | 255 929 | 30.71 | 385 976 | 34.04 | 520 388 | 36.33 |
| 3 persons | 141 736 | 17.00 | 188 895 | 16.66 | 227 008 | 15.85 |
| 4 persons | 152 159 | 18.26 | 191 091 | 16.85 | 222 767 | 14.75 |
| 5 persons | 81 839 | 9.82 | 89 159 | 7.86 | 91 188 | 6.42 |
| 6+ persons | 49 537 | 5.94 | 34 021 | 3.01 | 33 579 | 2.45 |
| Total | 833 503 | 100.00 | 1 133 775 | 100.00 | 1 441 582 | 100.00 |
| * Figures for 1996 and 2006 projected | | | | | | |

gentrification make to the socio-economic structure of a suburb?

e   Does your local government have area plans for future development? How would you like to see your local area develop?

## Brisbane's plan for urban renewal

A task force set up by the Brisbane City Council, with support from the Queensland government, is to plan for the future by redeveloping the north-eastern inner suburbs

The need for urban reform is based on

- high population growth in south-east Queensland
- population decline or stagnation in inner city areas
- changing social patterns
- obsolete land usage
- recognition of the costs of urban sprawl
- under-utilised physical and social infrastructure
- ill defined development directions
- non-viable commercial investments.

**8** Are these problems common to large cities in Australia? Discuss the problems of inner suburbs, as outlined above, in relation to your nearest large city. Are there any similar plans for urban renewal? If so, compare them with the plan for Brisbane.

**9** Look at the photograph, Figure 4.6. Make a field sketch of the area shown. Identify Brisbane's CBD, the Storey Bridge, the Brisbane River, industrial and residential areas.

**10** Answer these questions.

a   Can you co-ordinate the map, Figure 4.7 with the photograph, Figure 4.6? (Figure 4.8 should help you to do this.) What are the existing problems of this inner city area?

Figure 4.6 Inner north-eastern suburbs of Brisbane (Brisbane City Council)

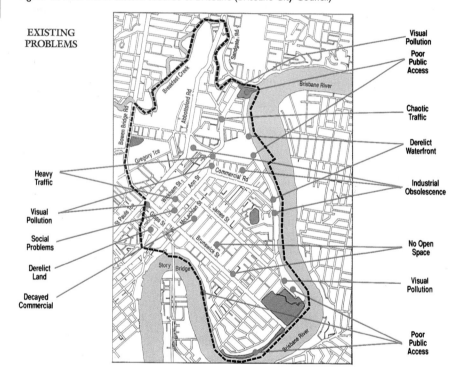

Figure 4.7 Existing problems

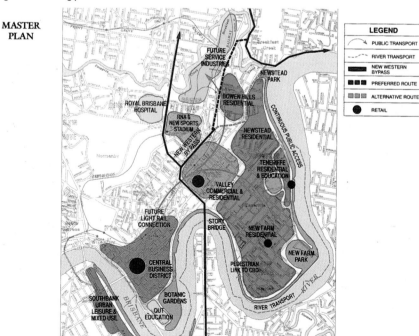

Figure 4.8 Master plan

| Table 4.4 Population, inner north-eastern suburbs of Brisbane | | | | | |
|---|---|---|---|---|---|
| Suburb | Area | Population | | Average | Proposed |
| | sq km | 1986 | 1991 | growth | population |
| Bowen Hills | 2 | 790 | 818 | 0.70 | 2 000 |
| Fortitude Valley | I | I 393 | I 320 | -1.07 | 7 000 |
| New Farm | 3 | 9 187 | 9 254 | 0.15 | II 000 |
| Newstead | 2 | I 048 | I 027 | -0.40 | 7 000 |
| Teneriffe | n/a | | | | 3 000 |
| Total | | 12 418 | 12 419 | | 30 000 |

On 19 July 1991, the Rt Hon Lord Mayor of Brisbane, Alderman Jim Soorley, with the support of Deputy Premier and Minister for housing and Local Government, the Hon Tom Burns M.L.A., appointed an Urban Renewal Task Force to investigate opportunities for urban renewal of the inner north-eastern suburbs of Brisbane.

The Task Force, representing private and public sectors, was required to identify practical solutions for legislative, financial and administrative aspects of urban renewal tofacilitate viable investments and affordable housing.

This report recommends a master plan, development strategies, and procedures for implementation, with detailed planning parameters, and highlights the following initiatives to achieve a population growth to 30,000 over the next 20 years:

- Strengthen employment opportunities to support a range of residential accommodation for all age brackets and walks of life.
- Revitalise Fortitude Valley as a major commercial centre, an exciting place to visit and a safe place to live.
- Redevelop Newstead as a new self-contained urban village within a highly pedestrianised and landscaped environment.
- Redevelop Teneriffe as a vibrant urban centre with residential, retail and education activities capitalising on the heritage of woolstores and water frontage.
- Consolidate New Farm as an established urban environment with an emphasis on the public consultation process.
- Discourage high-rise towers in residential precincts in favour of

creating low to medium-rise residential environments.
- Construct a new western bypass to stop heavy vehicle traffic passing through Fortitude Valley.
- Investigate impacts of special regulations and Gateway Bridge toll charges on heavy vehicles.
- Construct a new light rail system connecting all residential precincts to the CBD.
- Develop continuous public access to river frontages connecting Newstead Park, New Farm Park and Botanic Gardens.
- Convert Mayne railway yards into an attractive industry park.
- Expand the RNA to incorporate a multi purpose sports stadium.
- Relocate industries from waterfront locations and residential areas.
- Introduce financial incentives to stimulate development activity in the short term.
- Obtain funding to service low income housing and infrastructure costs of $250 million.
- Introduce imaginative demonstration projects for low income housing.
- Facilitate immediate implementation of catalyst projects.
- Adopt new legislation to streamline approval process for immediate development.
- Introduce mixed use zonings to provide a flexibility and improved viability of development projects.
- Create an administrative vehicle to ensure public consultation, joint venture participation, immediate implementation and responsibility for performance.

The Task Force emphasises that success of the project will depend upon the commitment of all levels of Government throughout the urban renewal process.

Figure 4.9 Task force initiatives

b Discuss the key features of the proposal shown on the master plan and the initiatives outlined by the task force. (See Table 4.4 and Figure 4.9.)

c Plans are under way to construct a twenty storey residential/retail/office building complex in Fortitude Valley. The task force is currently seeking public opinion about the proposal. Already 7000 objections have been raised about some of the plans for high density development, especially the building of townhouses and duplex dwellings on smaller than average sized blocks of land. These will not now be permitted in certain areas. Some of the objections were based on loss of quality of life by people living in prime residential areas and fears of increased traffic, noise and lack of privacy. If you were to respond to a similar plan in an urban area near you, what questions would you put to the task force?

## The Brisbane–Gold Coast population corridor

The southern sector of south–east Queensland is expected to dominate the population growth over the next decade.

II Think about South-east Queensland.

a What five LGAs are included in this part of Queensland?

b Which LGAs will have the greatest growth rate?

c By how many people will the area have increased by the year 2006?

d Discuss some of the pressures placed on the local governments in attempting to meet the demands of such a significant residential population increase.

e Not only is the residential population increasing but it is estimated that, in 2006, 100 000 more tourists a day than the 1986 number will visit the Gold Coast. What development/ infrastructure do you think will be needed to meet this increase?

With the increasing volumes of traffic between Brisbane and the Gold Coast it will be necessary for the main transport corridor to be upgraded to meet future demands. The major traffic link between Brisbane and the Gold Coast is the Pacific Highway which will not be able to cope with the increased traffic generated by the predicted population growth. Problems of traffic congestion are already occurring, with the road carrying an average of 50 000 vehicles a day, or 22.5 million person trips a year. The highway also carries ten million tonnes of freight a year. The traffic volume is expected to double by about the year 2001.

The big problem is how best to develop this transport corridor so that it can cope with future traffic volumes. The Eastern Corridor Planning Study (ECPS) was conducted by independent consultants to advise the state government on the best possible plan.

Some of the problems to be faced in developing the transport route are to

• minimise impacts on the lifestyle of residents

• plan noise abatement programs such as roadside embankments, vegetation buffers, thicker glass windows and insulation for houses along the route (doubling the Pacific Highway would increase noise levels by an estimated 10 to 15 per cent)

• avoiding increased air pollution through industrial and traffic emissions

• protect significant areas of bushland and existing koala habitats, especially north of the Logan River

• protect the wetland habitats south of the Logan River, near Lake Coombabah and other areas

• minimise the loss of cane lands in the area south of the Logan River

• take the highway across the Logan, Pimpama and Coomera Rivers so that the risk of upstream or downstream flooding is not increased by the developmental works

• co-ordinate a network of arterial and other road links to and through the LGAs through which the major highway will pass

• minimise the effect the physical barrier, created by the transport route, has on urban areas as it passes through LGAs such as Logan City.

A preferred route, from Beenleigh–Redland Road south to the Coomera River has been recommended to the government (see Figure 4.10). This route is one which provides for minimum impact on the residential, natural and agricultural environment of the areas through which it will pass. This transport corridor will be developed in stages in response to transport and population demands.

12 Think about transport.

a Why is it necessary to define the transport route even though it will be developed in stages in the future?

b What do you think would be the next stages in its development?

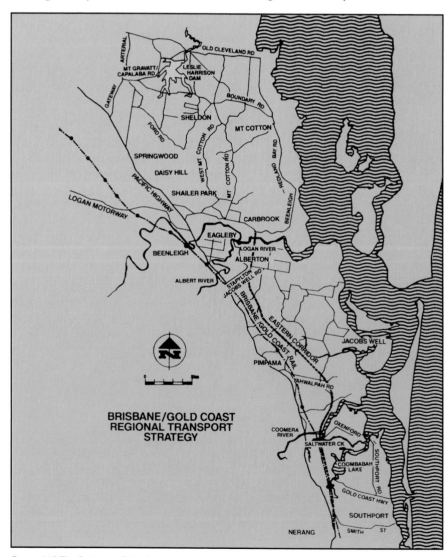

Figure 4.10 The Brisbane–Gold Coast transport corridor

In conjunction with the road transport link, work has already commenced on a plan to develop and expand the existing rail service by extending the rail line to Robina on the Gold Coast, build new stations and establish a fast rail service. With electric trains travelling up to 160 kilometres an hour this would provide a Brisbane/Robina journey of sixty-seven minutes. New stations will be co-ordinated with local bus services to carry passengers to Gold Coast beaches. It is estimated that more than three million passengers will use the upgraded rail service between Brisbane and the Gold Coast by the year 2000.

Large areas of both the natural and rural environment will be lost as development sprawls further out from existing urban boundaries. As urban areas expand outwards in response to population pressure it is often the rural land on the urban fringe which is threatened. Land prices reflect the value placed on the land and with urban expansion there is competition for the land from non-rural land users who can usually pay more for it. As the value of the land increases the farmer may also face increased rates and taxes and so the economic return from rural activities falls.

As the adjacent residential areas grow, residents may complain about day to day farming activities such as noise, dust, the use of chemicals, spray drift, cane burning etc., placing further restrictions on normal farming activities. The construction of infrastructure, such as freeways, can act as physical barriers which may lead to segregation of farming areas. This can lead to increased production costs and less efficient land use. 'Nearly a decade ago, U.S. Assistant Secretary of Agriculture, Robert

## POLICY PRINCIPLES

**1.** When preparing, reviewing or amending town planning schemes, local authorities will be expected to include provisions for the conservation of good quality agricultural land, regardless of the effect of market fluctuations on its viability.

**2.** The preparation of strategic plans should include an evaluation of alternative forms of development, and significant weight should be given to those strategies which minimise the impacts on good quality agricultural land.

**3.** Due consideration should be given to the protection of good quality agricultural land when applications for rezonings, consent, or subdivisions are being determined.

**4.** The alienation of some productive agricultural land will inevitably occur as a consequence of development, but the Government will not support such alienation when equally viable alternatives exist, particularly where developments that

do not have very specific locational requirements (e.g. 'rural residential') are involved.

**5.** The fact that existing farm units and smallholdings are not agriculturally viable does not in itself justify their further subdivision or rezoning for non-agricultural purposes. Nevertheless, subdivision polices should encourage amalgamation of titles where this would enhance farm viability.

**6.** Local authority planning provisions should aim to minimise instances of incompatible uses locating adjacent to agricultural operations in a manner that inhibits normal farming practice. Where such instances do arise, measures to ameliorate potential conflicts should be devised wherever practicable.

**7.** Where a town planning scheme does not contain adequate provisions, the Government will be guided by the principles set out in this bulletin when considering applications for rezoning or amendments to town planning schemes.

Figure 4.11 Queensland government policy principles for agricultural land development and conservation

Cutler, observed that 'asphalt is the land's last crop.' Once productive cropland is lost to suburban development, shopping malls, or roads, it is difficult to restore it to food production.'[2]

---

**13** Do you agree with this quotation? Is there any evidence of rural land being lost to urban development in your area? Discuss.

---

Some countries have definite controls over cropland, for example, Japan has put land into three categories—industrial, agricultural and other. It is illegal to build on cropland. California, USA and Ontario, Canada also have strict controls over agricultural land resources.[3]

---

**14** Should we have similar laws? Should there be greater control over rural and other land near urban centres? Discuss.

Control of land use in Queensland is in the hands of local authorities, who at times need to make decisions so that there is a balance between development and conservation. Government guidelines have been provided to assist local authorities in decision making concerning rural land. (See Figure 4.11.)

The Queensland government's concern about land conservation is expressed in a position statement

*…The best and most versatile farming land has a special importance and should not be built on unless there is an over-riding need for the development in terms of public benefit and no other site is suitable for the particular purpose. This land is a valuable resource that should, in general, be protected from irreversible development. In such cases, additional weight needs to be given to the agriculture factor.*

The Government considers that good quality agricultural land is a finite national and state resource that must be conserved and managed for the longer term. As a general aim, the exercise of town planning powers should be used to protect such land from those developments that lead to its alienation or diminished productivity. [4]

15 The position statement outlined above indicates the value that the Queensland government places on the preservation of agricultural land.

a   What happens if a community places greater value on certain areas of the natural environment and prefers development to take place on agricultural land in the area?

b   How do you identify those areas that should be preserved and those most suitable for development?

c   In what ways do you think development planning differs from conservation planning?

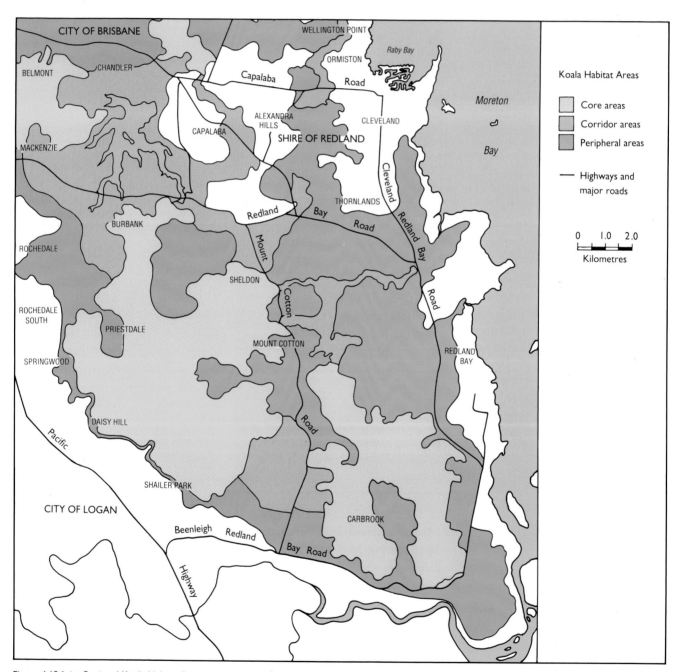

Figure 4.12 Joint Regional Koala Habitat Project

## Redland Shire: Planning for the future

Redland Shire, located in the rapidly developing urban corridor of the south-east, is one of Queensland's fastest growing areas.

---

**16** Answer these questions.
a   Identify the location of Redland Shire on the map, Figure 4.3. What local authorities does it adjoin?
b   What is its estimated growth rate? (See Table 4.2.)
c   What is its estimated population in the year 2001?
d   Where are the major urban areas of Redland Shire? Use Figure 4.12 to answer this question.

---

Redland Shire, which includes North Stradbroke and other Moreton Bay islands, was once a very important horticultural area but has more recently developed as a dormitory suburb of Brisbane. Urban development is now encroaching onto the remaining agricultural and bushland areas. Without a firm planning policy over the next few years urban development could take place across the whole shire. Urban development of neighbouring LGAs has, in many cases, reached Redland's boundary and is bordering important bushland and koala habitat areas. (See Figure 4.12.)

Without adequate safeguards urban development could push further into these areas.

In general, urban planning is for development purposes and at times, this has been at the expense of the natural environment and sensitive habitats. The remaining 'left over' land, usually small and fragmented, is then the only option for the creation of environmental or open space.

When the Leslie Harrison Dam was constructed about ten years ago its main purpose was to provide a water supply for future urban development. As part of the scheme it was necessary to preserve an area of 85 square kilometres of bushland as a catchment to ensure adequate water runoff into the dam. It was a developmental rather than an environmental decision. However, the catchment is now one of the few substantially intact bushland areas still surviving, and it is one of Australia's most important koala habitats.

Without adequate planning, conflict can occur as development takes place in what is discovered to be an environmentally sensitive area. It is not necessarily the fault of developers but results through not identifying the sensitive areas in advance and having appropriate protection mechanisms. Conflict between developers, conservationists, governments, farmers, business and other groups and individuals is costly, time consuming, and generally results in a compromise solution.

Redland Shire has the last significant areas of lowland bushland in south-east Queensland. This bushland is also one of the most important koala habitats remaining in Australia. The council is committed to the on-going preservation of the bushland and sees existing cleared land (which includes agricultural land) as the basis for future urban development.

The dilemma is how to protect agricultural land as outlined in the government planning criteria and balance conservation and open space needs with urban growth. If state government policy is to be followed the remaining agricultural land should have a higher priority for preservation than the bushland.

---

**17** Consider the information you have just read.
a   Which would be your choice? Give some reasons.
b   How would you resolve the dilemma?

Figure 4.13a Lowland bushland habitat, Redlands. The tree in the photograph is sp. *Eucalyptus tereticoris*. Can you spot the koala? (Gary White, Redland Shire Council)

Figure 4.13b 'Are you going to destroy my habitat?' (John Mason)

Redlands and adjoining bushland areas provide an opportunity to preserve a major habitat adjacent to a large metropolitan area. However, some people think that being close to Brisbane, the urban development potential is more important because there are koala habitats in other areas.

**18** What do you think? How can this habitat be kept intact? What would you do about these environmentally sensitive areas? Discuss.

In planning for habitat and conservation needs, the important thing is to identify environmentally sensitive issues in advance. The most important areas could be protected as national or environmental parks, but as land acquisition can be very costly other options are also needed. Protection mechanisms and associated management by-laws, such as a tree protection by-law, must also be part of the planning process. Planning should provide maximum opportunity for the community, now and in the future, to be able to make choices among alternative strategies and across a range of issues. Since political boundaries may cross important habitat and conservation areas, planning should also be part of an overall regional plan.

**19** Look at the map, Figure 4.12.
a Where are the most important koala habitats in Redlands?
b Other areas have been identified and marked on the map.
What is a corridor area? What is its major function? What type of areas could be suitable for this purpose? Do you have any environmental corridors in your local area?

c What is a peripheral area?
d In looking at the map, where do you think development should take place? What other information would you need to make such a decision?

What provisions has Redlands made for habitat protection?
*i)Council has amended the Strategic Plan following vegetation survey and analysis to include intact bushland areas in the southern part of the shire as being of habitat significance. By taking this action, Council has, in effect, put on notice that in considering any future land uses, the habitat significance issue will be taken into account in the process.*
*ii)Following the success of the Leslie Harrison Dam Catchment for water supply purposes, the Redland Shire Council has followed this by designating the significant vegetation area as a new zoning within the Town Plan—Habitat/Water Supply Significance.*
*★ Both of the areas in i and ii have been complemented by the introduction of specific tree preservation measures.*
*iii) . . . work has reached an advanced stage for the introduction of Development Control Plan amendments in which development is provided for, provided such development accords with habitat protection provisions which have been outlined as objectives.*
*iv)Other provisions of the scheme prohibit removal of vegetation in associated areas allocated for urban purposes prior to approval being received by Council to enable Council to make assessment of habitat opportunities in association with park areas and corridor systems.* [5]

You may argue that Queensland is a large state with plenty of space, but in reality only 2 per cent of the land can be regarded as cropland and 1.6 per cent of this is currently under crops. Because most of this land is located along the east coast it is, in many places, already being lost through urban expansion. The loss of sugar cane farmland is one example.

**20** Use Table 4.5 and Figure 4.15.
a How much cane land has been lost for urban or other agricultural use in the last decade?
b Which mills lost the largest areas of cane land to urban, infrastructure and other non-agricultural use? Make allowance for the area assigned to cane which has been transferred to new cane growing land.
c What large urban areas are located in the same areas in which sugar cane is grown? Are these also areas of urban growth? (See also Figure 4.14.)

**RESEARCH TOPIC 4.1**

Complete either question (a) or question (b).
a In recent years development issues have occurred in Queensland. These have been related to the loss of a specific habitat as well as sensitive mangrove areas. (A habitat issue resulting from mining activities is included in Chapter 5). Look for issues that may be reported in the media. What is the issue? Has it been resolved? What was the result?
b Have you had any examples of conflict over development in your local area? What were the issues? How was the conflict resolved?

# Table 4.5 Assigned cane land transferred to other uses, 1980–90

| Mill | A ha | B ha | C ha | D ha | E km | Mill | A ha | B ha | C ha | D ha | E km |
|---|---|---|---|---|---|---|---|---|---|---|---|
| Mossman | 434 | 0 | 364 | 464 | 28 | Pleystowe | 0 | 27 | 502 | 345 | 20 |
| *Hambledon | 1574 | 16 | 170 | 85 | 25 | Marian | 0 | 0 | 434 | 394 | 11 |
| Mulgrave | 282 | 0 | 0 | 0 | - | Cattle Creek | 0 | 0 | 175 | 106 | 15 |
| Babinda | 0 | 0 | 1135 | 0 | - | Plane Creek | 0 | 5 | 1580 | 1440 | 25 |
| Mourilyan | 70 | 3 | 720 | 0 | - | Fairymead | 95 | 0 | 826 | 481 | 21 |
| South Johnstone | 0 | 0 | 400 | 60 | 8 | Millaquin | 0 | 12 | 886 | 792 | 21 |
| Tully | 0 | 0 | 45 | 45 | 8.7 | Bingera | 0 | 12 | 1380 | 976 | 19 |
| Macknade | 0 | 0 | 227 | 202 | 16 | Isis | 0 | 25 | 0 | 0 | - |
| Victoria | 0 | 0 | 306 | 306 | 26 | Maryborough | 61 | 19 | 866 | 912 | 20 |
| Invicta | 0 | 0 | 197 | 197 | 40 | Moreton | 133 | 110 | 335 | 100 | 25 |
| Pioneer | 0 | 0 | 180 | 180 | 11 | Rocky Point | 0 | 11 | 360 | 35 | 7 |
| Kalamia | 48 | 0 | 8 | 36 | 7 | Condong | 163 | 234 | 2 | 0 | - |
| Inkerman | 2 | 0 | 20 | 22 | 10 | Broadwater | 150 | 0 | 1190 | 1340 | 26 |
| Proserpine | 200 | 4 | 0 | 200 | 27 | Harwood | 51 | 100 | 589 | 740 | 32 |
| Farleigh | 516 | 4 | 576 | 703 | 39 | **Total** | **3882** | **615** | **13743** | **10285** | |
| Racecourse | 103 | 33 | 270 | 124 | 23 | | | | | | |

A = Area of assigned cane land rezoned to non-rural uses.

B = Area of assigned cane land resumed or purchased by government body for roads, railways, schools etc.

C = Area of assigned cane land lost to other uses in rural zone e.g. hobby farms, other agriculture or special uses.

D = Area of assignment from A, B & C transferred to new land.

E = Average distance of reassigned land from Mill.

\* The Hambledon mill closed at the end of the 1991 crushing season

Note: 'assigned cane land' is a particular area of land where sugar cane is grown for delivery to a particular mill. Assignments are regulated by the Queensland Sugar Corporation

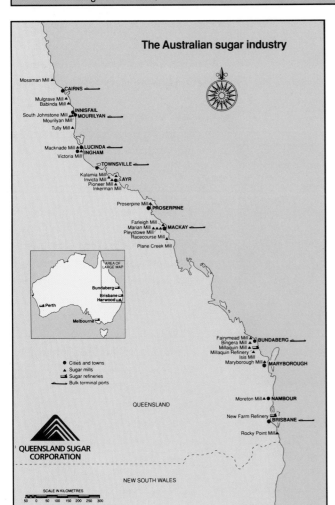

Figure 4.14 Sugar mills, location

Figure 4.15 Urban development takes over the cane fields near Cairns

## RESEARCH TOPIC 4.2

Does your LGA have a town plan? What provision does it make for habitat protection? What provision does it make for tree preservation? (For many urban areas where past development has destroyed most of the natural environment such planning may not be a choice.)

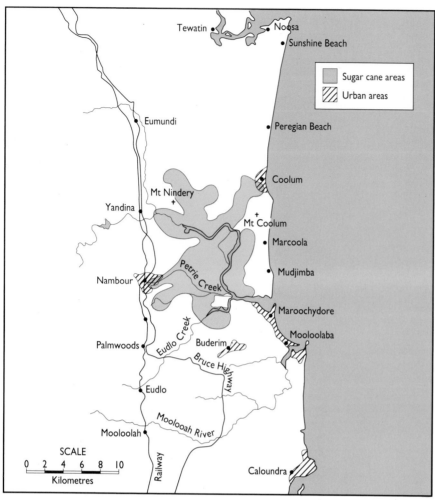

Figure 4.16 The Sunshine Coast

Figure 4.17 Sugar cane farms, the Sunshine Coast

| Table 4.6 Population growth, the Sunshine Coast | | | | | | | |
|---|---|---|---|---|---|---|---|
| L G A | 1966 | 1971 | 1976 | 1981 | 1986 | 1991 | 2006 |
| Noosa | 6 673 | 7 746 | 9 280 | 14 640 | 18 770 | 26 259 | 45 178 |
| Maroochy | 21 455 | 25 522 | 34 890 | 50 940 | 61 050 | 77 945 | 126 524 |
| Caloundra | 8 798 | 11 314 | 15 720 | 26 600 | 35 940 | 50 669 | 94 001 |
| Total | 36 926 | 44 582 | 59 890 | 92 180 | 115 760 | 154 883 | 265 703 |

## Case study: The Sunshine Coast and the sugar industry.

Sugar cane is grown on alluvial land in stream valleys and coastal lowlands on the Sunshine Coast, in the Shires of Maroochydore and Noosa and Caloundra City. The region has a very attractive coast and hinterland and is one of the fastest growing areas in south–east Queensland with an estimated population of over 265 000 by the year 2006. The cane land is close to a number of rapidly growing urban areas where there is growing pressure for rural land to be used for housing, industry, tourism and public use as well as accompanying infrastructure such as freeways and highways. Cane land has already been lost to residential and tourist development as well as for upgrading and diversions of the Bruce Highway. Further development of the Sunshine Coast Motorway, which will be extended from Maroochydore to Noosa, will result in the loss of more cane land. The importance of the sugar industry to the Sunshine Coast is outlined in the open letter from the manager of the Moreton Mill, Figure 4.18.

21 Look at the map of the Sunshine Coast, Figure 4.16.

a Identify the cane growing areas, urban areas, and major transport routes.

b Look at the vertical aerial photograph taken on 23 June 1991, Figure 4.19 and the map, Figure 4.20. Identify the following on the photograph

 • Twin Waters Resort and golf course
 • Sunshine Coast Airport
 • Sunshine Motorway
 • cane rail tracks
 • canal residential development.

c Note that two areas were being developed at the time the photograph was taken. At C/D-4/5, this is now a new residential area. Can you identify the new road developed at F-2/3?

# Sugar vital to economy

### Graham Coleman. Moreton Mill

Moreton Mill was established in 1896 under the Works Guarantee Act and has operated at the current site in Nambour since that time.

The mill currently crushes cane grown on some 7334 hectares of land on the Sunshine Coast.

In 1991, the mill crushed over 500,000 tonnes of cane, producing 71,000 tonnes of raw sugar, a record for the mill.

The direct value of the 1991 production to the Sunshine Coast will be more than $22 million.

Over the last 10 years, more than $16 million has been invested in upgrading plant at Moreton Mill. This has involved local trade contractors, creating additional jobs over that involved in annual sugar production.

The majority of expenditure during the past three years was on new equipment for the manufacture of special raw sugars, particularly industrial and food grade sugars.

The diversification will enhance the economic strength of the mill through value adding and increase the contribution of the sugar industry to the regional economy.

The recent takeover of Bundaberg Sugar Company by Tate and Lyle signals a strong and continued growth for Moreton Mill.

Being close to a major metropolitan market, Moreton Mill is well placed to expand its production of food grade sugar.

Taking into account the multiplier effects which flow through a wide range of businesses and industries on the Coast, it has been calculated that the Coast sugar industry will have been responsible for more than $45 million of regional output in 1991 and $70 million of national output.

Total direct and indirect employment associated with the sugar industry in the Coast region is over 700 persons.

The sugar industry is one which meets the needs of the Coast for sustainable economic development.

In a community which attaches significant value to environment matters, the extent to which the sugar industry operates as a closed loop in relation to energy consumption is important.

All by-products have uses and there are no waste products of a toxic nature. Research indicates that the industry can be regarded as 'Green House Gas' neutral, returning the same amount of carbon dioxide to the atmosphere as it drew from it originally.

The sugar industry in the region has the capacity to continue to expand provided the valuable agricultural land on which the industry depends is protected.

Cane farming can only continue in the region if there is sufficient production to maintain the viability of the sugar mill must continue to increase its throughput of sugar, aiming for a target of at least 80,000 tonnes of sugar a year within the next 10 years.

Unlike many other primary industries, it is not possible to transport cane to a manufacturing plant outside the region. This is because of the high cost of transporting cane relative to the product value. It takes almost eight tonnes of cane to produce one tonne of sugar.

There is a very limited stock of land suitable for cane growing in the region. However, with appropriate land-use policies which aim to conserve our limited valuable cropland, the sugar industry can remain a powerful part of economic growth in the region.

Figure 4.18

Figure 4.19 Vertical aerial photograph—Maroochy River area 1991

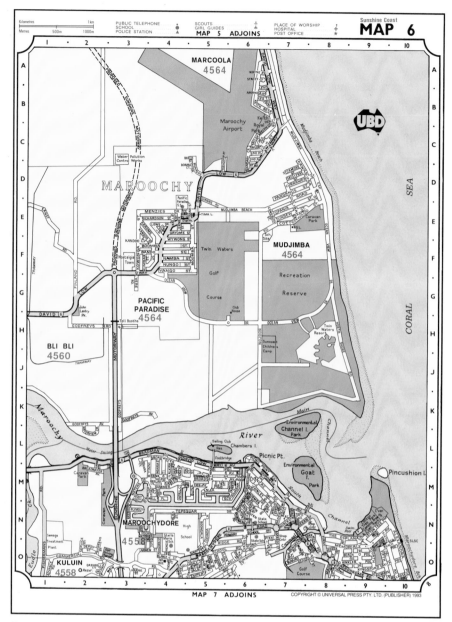

Figure 4.20 The Maroochy River area

d Using a photocopy of Map D, page 90, mark in or shade the following
  • areas of mangroves/wetlands
  • canefields
  • residential areas (use arrows to indicate in which direction you think that they may possibly expand in the future).

e Can you identify areas of cane land already being isolated by residential or other development? Is cane land threatened?

Because of the projected population growth of the Sunshine Coast over the next decade, developers are always on the lookout for prime development sites. Recently, a representative of a large company offered the owner of a cane farm a much higher price than could be obtained by selling it as a farming property. He has accepted their offer subject to the land being re-zoned. The current owner is a third generation cane farmer, the land being acquired by his grandfather earlier this century. He is planning to live in retirement on the money obtained from the sale of the 40 hectare farm as his family, now grown-up, are not interested in taking over the property. His only income is from the sale of cane and so he sees the valuable property as his superannuation package. He also claims that as he has freehold title to the property it is his right to dispose of the farm as he chooses. He is concerned that competition from overseas cane growing countries, and pending government de-regulation of the sugar industry, offer an uncertain future for cane growers and that many cane farmers may have no alternative but to sell their land.

Three councillors have to consider the application for re-zoning of the land. Although Maroochy Shire policy is to protect cane land from unnecessary development this policy is not always maintained—as is evident from past sub-divisions of cane land for housing estates. Local authorities do not always have the last word on re-zoning. In 1988, the Maroochy Shire Council and the Moreton Sugar Company Inc., opposed the re-zoning of some 81 hectares of cane land for residential use. The Local Government Court (a state court of appeal) ruled in favour of the developer and the land was re-zoned.

The decision of the local councillors will be based on the arguments contained in the various submissions and what they see to be in the best interests of the whole area. (See Figure 4.11 for state government guidelines.)

The notice of the proposed re-development scheme has been announced and the local council has called for comments on the plan from residents, professional organisations and landowners. Plans for the site are being developed and will be available for public comment for one month prior to a council decision being made.

Groups of people plan to protest about the proposed sale of the farm for residential purposes. Others are in favour of the proposed redevelopment of the land.

**The developers** have applied to the local council for approval to re-zone and develop the land. The development proposes a wide range of residential dwellings, including cluster or integrated housing on small subdivisions, traditional dwellings, medium density apartments and town houses. As the land has a river frontage, some canal development is desirable to provide waterfront properties and enhance the area. Development would follow the 'Green Street' concept which is supported by state and federal governments. Ten per cent of the total area would be allocated to recreation space, including public gardens, pedestrian walkways, bike ways, children's play areas and general recreation space. Public access to the river front would also be made available. The developers stress that the project will meet strict environmental guidelines. They also

highlight the benefits to the community of the employment opportunities during the building stage. To support their application they cite other cases where cane land has recently been re-zoned for residential development.

The developers are supported by a number of small business people and others who see the development as an opportunity for growth. The area is about an hour's drive from Brisbane and completion of the freeway, north to Noosa, will encourage further development. They also argue that it is only a matter of time before the south-east of Queensland is the second largest urban area in Queensland, so a change in land use on the Sunshine Coast is inevitable. Any delay in development plans will add substantial costs to the project.

**The employees** represent the Moreton Sugar Company Limited, mill employees and some cane farmers, as well as associated businesses. The mill owners want to maintain the economic viability of the mill. With local unemployment levels already high the employees can see no prospects for alternative

employment if the mill is forced to close. The employees are supported by many others as the town is very dependent on the money and employment that is both directly and indirectly a result of the mill activities. The loss of cane land not only affects the mill but has a great impact on the whole region.

**A local resident** action group represents a number of concerned residents. They maintain that the cane farm is part of the human environment that contributes to the scenic and diversified nature of the area. The lifestyle is what attracted many people to the area. The residents want to see the current balance of urban/rural maintained and do not want to see it change, as has happened in other areas. They are concerned that the current pace of urbanisation and the projected population growth of the area in the next decade or so may lead to a scramble by developers for land. They use the Gold Coast as one example of urban development that they do not want. They also argue that development should first take place closer to the larger established urban areas and so minimise the urban sprawl which is already taking place.

**Another group of people** see this proposed development as an opportunity to express their concern for what is happening to the local environment. They prefer the land to remain rural rather than be re-zoned residential. Their policy is to rehabilitate and protect parts of the area where possible and thus provide a better environment for the future. One project focuses on the Maroochy River system and ways to preserve it in an unpolluted state. They want to have input into any development scheme that may affect the Maroochy River and adjoining areas.

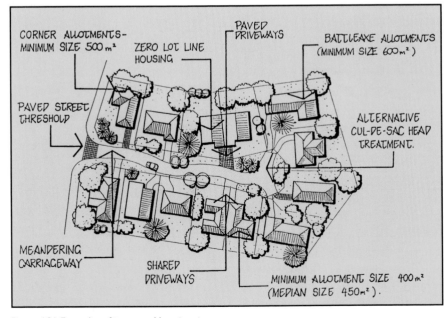

Figure 4.21 Examples of integrated housing

The Maroochy River is one of the few rivers along the east coast of Queensland that enters the sea through its natural outlet. One issue that concerns environmentalists is the destruction of mangroves that has taken place in areas along the river bank. Environmentalists highlight the importance of mangroves to the river ecosystems and are pressing for a buffer zone to be developed between farms and the river. Where the river banks have been cleared they could be re-planted with mangroves to protect the river bank and to provide a natural habitat for river and bird life. One wetlands park is currently being developed near the site and residential development could have an effect on it.

**22** Role play

a **Select roles.** Three class members will act as the councillors. The rest of the class will divide into four groups, one for each of the interest groups outlined. Roles may be allocated by ballot or choice, the class can decide. Each member of a group should identify with an appropriate role—cane farmer, mill worker, resident, etc. Each group could also decide on a group name and acronym—'Friends of Mangroves' (FOMs).

b **Prepare submissions.** Councillors and members of the four groups will first become familiar with the general area and the way that it has developed. Collect evidence that will both highlight each group's case as well as show the weaknesses of the alternatives.
Draw from information in this chapter or use examples of what has happened in similar cases in your local area or other areas. Your arguments should highlight the benefits to both the environment of the area and the community and in doing so consider the concept of 'sustainable development'. You may seek support from other groups, prepare newspaper statements/posters for publicity purposes.

c) **Present the submission.** On a given date you will present your submission to the council. All groups will have the same time allowed for this and a spokesperson for each group will highlight the key points in the submission. Councillors must be fully aware of all the issues so that they are best prepared to make an informed decision. After all the submissions have been presented the councillors will give their decision. Will the decision made today also be in the best interests of future generations?

While the south-east and other Queensland urban areas are expanding to meet the needs of an increasing population other areas are facing a different problem.

In recent years rural areas of Queensland have not only had to battle against drought, flood and the economic recession but also the drift of the population to urban areas and the decline of the small towns which are so important to rural communities. It is not uncommon to drive into once prosperous towns to see empty shops, closed down railway stations and indications of the loss of services such as provided by banks, law courts and government authorities. One reason for the loss of services is accessibility, because of better roads and cars, to nearby larger urban areas where people have a wider range of goods and services from which to choose. Another reason is the movement of people, in retirement, to nearby larger urban areas where there are more facilities and services available for them. For example, the town of Dalby (population 9737) has had zero population growth since 1986. Toowoomba, with an average annual growth rate of 1.40 per cent, lies only 83 kilometres away.

**23** If you lived in Dalby what are some things that you may travel to Toowoomba for? How long would it take to cover the distance?

**24** Use Fig 4.1 and Tables 4.2 and 4.6.

a Can you suggest other reasons why some small towns are in decline?
b Which of the Queensland statistical divisions are showing an outflow of population? Most of the shires in the South-west, Central West and North-west have negative or very low average growth rates.
c Where is the population outflow headed?
d Is it important that small towns continue to exist?
How can they be helped to survive?

| Table 4.7 Western statistical division, population | | | |
|---|---|---|---|
| Statistical division | 1986 | 1991 | Average growth rate 1986–91 |
| South-west | 28 699 | 28 611 | -0.06 |
| Central West | 13 585 | 13 098 | -0.73 |
| North-west | 38 601 | 38 386 | -0.11 |

**End notes**
1 *The Eastern Corridor Planning Study* (ECPS) (1992), Rankine & Hill, Brisbane
2 Coleman, G. and Edwards, L.D. (1991) 'Management of arable land resources', Proc. of Aust.Soc.of Sugar Cane Technol., p. 20
3 Coleman and Edwards, pp. 19–20
4 Dept. of Housing and Local Govt./Qld Dept. of Primary Industries. (May 1991) 'Development and the Conservation of Agricultural Land'. *Planning Bulletin* No. 1/91, pp. 1 and 2
5 Gary White, Shire Planner, *Planning for Habitat and Conservation Needs in South East Queensland: A Case Study*, Redland Shire Council

# Chapter 5

# QUEENSLAND'S RESOURCES

## What is a resource?

For many people their perception of a resource is often related to coal, iron ore or other minerals. Is this your perception of a resource? Put simply, a resource is a means of supplying a need. In a modern state such as Queensland, resources are used to both provide for peoples' needs and to generate wealth. We may use the resource directly or indirectly. For example, black coal can be used to produce the electrical power needed by society. By exporting black coal overseas part of the money gained through taxes or royalties paid to government authorities can go towards providing services and infrastructure for the community.

Figure 5.1 Some Queensland resources

1 Look at the photographs, Figure 5.1. What resources can you identify in each photograph? Give reasons for your answer.

Resources are linked to the stage of technological development of a country. Black coal was not a resource for the Queensland Aborigines because they were unaware of its uses and also lacked the technology needed for mining and processing it.

2 Can you name some resources that would have been used by Aborigines before European settlement?

Resources can also be identified as being renewable or non-renewable. The products made from some non-renewable resources can be recycled.

3 Answer these questions.
a Can you think of a resource that can be used over and over again?
b Which such resource is visible in the photographs, Figure 5.1?
c Some resources can only be used once. Do any of these appear in the photographs?
When you complete this chapter have another look at the photographs and see if you can identify some more resources.
d Can you give some examples of recyclable products made from non-renewable resources? What are some benefits of recycling products made from non-renewable resources?

Have you thought of people as a resource? Before reading more of this chapter perhaps you could have a class discussion using the following questions as guidelines.

## People as a resource

4 Think about people.
a In what way are people a resource?
b Are human resources renewable or non-renewable? Explain.
c It is often said that 'children are our greatest resource'. Have you thought of yourself as a resource? In what way?
d It is also said that children should be given the best education possible so that they are well prepared to meet the needs of society in the future. In what way is education linked with the concept of you as a resource?
e Frequent comment in the media refers to the need for Australia to become a 'clever country'. What does this mean and what has it to do with human resources?
f In what way is a high rate of unemployment an under-utilisation of resources?

g Can a country be rich in human resources but poor in natural resources? How could it best utilise the human resources that it has? How can it overcome the lack of natural resources? Can you give an example?

h How can a country rich in natural resources, but lacking technological skills, develop its natural resources in the present and in the future? Can you give examples?

i Queensland is rich in natural resources but has not always had the human resources required to fully develop these. What attempts have been made to resolve this?

## Mineral resources

In this section the term minerals is used in a very broad sense, referring to those resources of economic value which are extracted from the earth.

Queensland is one of the largest mineral producing states in Australia and the mining industry is of importance to both Queensland as a state and to Australia as a nation.

5 Look at Tables 5.1 and 5.2.
a In terms of value which are the major minerals produced in Queensland?
b Which minerals show increases in productivity?
c Do increases in quantity also correlate with increases in value?

## Gold

In Chapter 3 reference was made to the contribution gold mining made to the social and economic structure of Queensland last century. The gold miners at that time were seeking alluvial gold or gold deposits located close to the surface. Mining methods were labour intensive and relatively simple. Towards the end of the century, as the alluvial and more easily worked gold deposits were rapidly exhausted, expensive shaft mining and processing methods became necessary. Mining for gold today is capital intensive using highly technical and complex processes for crushing and amalgamating or smelting to extract the gold which is alloyed with other metals. Kidston, one of Queensland's important gold mines, was re-opened in 1985. The gold is mined using the open-cut method.

Gold represents stored wealth—more than half of the gold ever produced lies in secure vaults in various places around the world.

6 Questions about gold.
a The quantity of gold production in Queensland has increased over the past ten years. Is this also true for its value? Where does gold rank, in value, compared with other minerals?
b Look at Tables 5.1 and 5.2. Is there any relationship between the price of gold and the production of gold? Construct a composite line/column graph. Use a column graph for production and a line graph for price. Calculate your own scale or use a vertical scale of 1cm: $100 million on the right side of the graph and a vertical scale of 1cm:10 000 kg on the left side.
c How much is the world price for gold today? Check the gold price (in the financial pages of newspapers and often on the television news) for a short period of time and then draw a graph to show any variation in its price.
d If the price of gold is high what effects could this have on an existing gold mine and on a gold mining company? What could happen if the price of gold drops sharply?
e Where is gold mined in Queensland? Use Figure 5.2 to answer this question.
f Which of these are also the places where past gold mining activities occurred?
g Why do you think that renewed mining activities have taken place in these old gold mining areas?
h Queensland is Australia's second largest gold producer. Which state produces the most gold?

**Table 5.1 Queensland mineral production, quantity**

| Mineral | 1985–86 | 1986–87 | 1987–88 | 1988–89 | 1989–90 | 1990–91 |
|---|---|---|---|---|---|---|
| Black coal ('000 tonnes) | 68 996 | 68 820 | 65 819 | 74 118 | 74 931 | 78 363 |
| Crude oil (megalitres) | 1 687 | 1 799 | 1 612 | 1 518 | 1 416 | 1 242 |
| Natural gas (gigalitres) | 505 | 546 | 620 | 600 | 636 | 938 |
| Copper ore and concentrate ('000 tonnes) | 637 | 692 | 616 | 690 | 745 | 741 |
| Bauxite ('000 tonnes) | 7 170 | 7 893 | 8 449 | 9 548 | 10 049 | 11 401 |
| Lead ore and concentrate ('000 tones) | 425 | 351 | 362 | 345 | 363 | 421 |
| Gold* (kg) | 18 622 | 23 287 | 36 168 | 46 743 | 51 730 | 43 954 |
| Zinc concentrate ('000 tonnes) | 383 | 414 | 357 | 339 | 349 | 442 |
| Mineral sands ('000 tonnes) | 379 | 509 | 464 | 479 | 396 | 321 |

* Includes bullion and alluvial.
Sources: ABS, Mineral Production Australia; ABS, Mineral production Queensland; Queensland Department of Resource Industries

**Table 5.2 Queensland mineral production, value ($ m)**

| Mineral | 1985–86 | 1986–87 | 1987–88 | 1988–89 | 1989–90 |
|---|---|---|---|---|---|
| Black coal | 2668 | 2673 | 2145 | 2381 | 2831 |
| Crude oil | 345 | 269 | 210 | 115 | 121 |
| Natural gas | 37 | 44 | 40 | 39 | 47 |
| Copper ore and concentrate | 251 | 297 | 410 | 527 | 564 |
| Bauxite | 161 | 170 | 186 | 206 | 238 |
| Lead ore and concentrate | 147 | 161 | 213 | 161 | 214 |
| Gold* | 172 | 254 | 396 | 470 | 523 |
| Zinc concentrate | 62 | 90 | 77 | 154 | 168 |
| Mineral sands | 58 | 85 | 89 | 122 | 121 |
| Other | 104 | 126 | 140 | 209 | 232 |
| Total | 4005 | 4169 | 3906 | 4384 | 5059 |

* Includes bullion and alluvial.
Sources: Queensland Department of Resource Industries

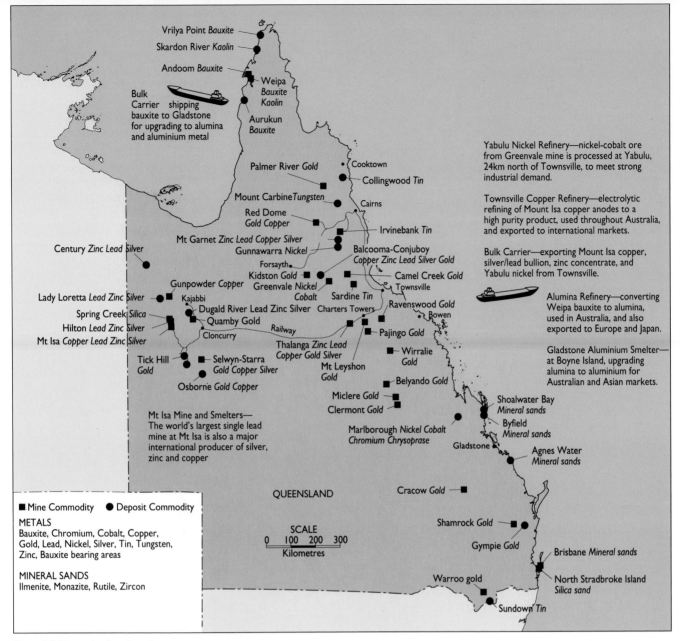

Figure 5.2 Queensland's minerals

The labels on the map, from top to bottom and left to right, include:

Vrilya Point *Bauxite*
Skardon River *Kaolin*
Andoom *Bauxite*
Bulk Carrier shipping bauxite to Gladstone for upgrading to alumina and aluminium metal
Weipa *Bauxite Kaolin*
Aurukun *Bauxite*
Palmer River *Gold*
Cooktown
Collingwood *Tin*
Mount Carbine *Tungsten*
Cairns
Red Dome *Gold Copper*
Irvinebank *Tin*
Mt Garnet *Zinc Lead Copper Silver*
Gunnawarra *Nickel*
Balcooma-Conjuboy *Copper Zinc Lead Silver Gold*
Century *Zinc Lead Silver*
Forsayth
Kidston *Gold*
Greenvale *Nickel*
Camel Creek *Gold*
Townsville
Gunpowder *Copper*
Kajabbi
Sardine *Tin*
Charters Towers
Ravenswood *Gold*
Bowen
Lady Loretta *Lead Zinc Silver*
Dugald River Lead Zinc Silver
Quamby Gold
Cloncurry
Railway
Pajingo *Gold*
Spring Creek *Silica*
Hilton *Lead Zinc Silver*
Mt Isa *Copper Lead Zinc Silver*
Thalanga *Zinc Lead Copper Gold Silver*
Wirralie *Gold*
Tick Hill *Gold*
Selwyn-Starra *Gold Copper Silver*
Mt Leyshon *Gold*
Belyando *Gold*
Osborne *Gold Copper*
Miclere *Gold*
Shoalwater Bay *Mineral sands*
Clermont *Gold*
Byfield *Mineral sands*
Marlborough *Nickel Cobalt Chromium Chrysoprase*
Gladstone
Agnes Water *Mineral sands*
Mt Isa Mine and Smelters—The world's largest single lead mine at Mt Isa is also a major international producer of silver, zinc and copper
Cracow *Gold*
QUEENSLAND
SCALE
0 100 200 300
Kilometres
Shamrock *Gold*
Gympie *Gold*
Brisbane *Mineral sands*
North Stradbroke Island *Silica sand*
Warroo gold
Sundown *Tin*

Yabulu Nickel Refinery—nickel-cobalt ore from Greenvale mine is processed at Yabulu, 24km north of Townsville, to meet strong industrial demand.

Townsville Copper Refinery—electrolytic refining of Mount Isa copper anodes to a high purity product, used throughout Australia, and exported to international markets.

Bulk Carrier—exporting Mount Isa copper, silver/lead bullion, zinc concentrate, and Yabulu nickel from Townsville.

Alumina Refinery—converting Weipa bauxite to alumina, used in Australia, and also exported to Europe and Japan.

Gladstone Aluminium Smelter—at Boyne Island, upgrading alumina to aluminium for Australian and Asian markets.

■ Mine Commodity   ● Deposit Commodity

METALS
Bauxite, Chromium, Cobalt, Copper, Gold, Lead, Nickel, Silver, Tin, Tungsten, Zinc, Bauxite bearing areas

MINERAL SANDS
Ilmenite, Monazite, Rutile, Zircon

Figure 5.3a Mt Morgan 1906

Gold mining began in Mt Morgan in 1886 and the mine was closed in 1990. Mt Morgan was also the second largest copper deposit in Queensland.

**7** Look at the photograph of Mt Morgan mine in 1906, Figure 5.3a.

a Make a field sketch of the photograph. The smoke-stacks are part of the various powerhouses. Name two types of fuel which would probably have been used in the powerhouses. The buildings on the left are the batteries where the ore was crushed.

b How is the waste material (tailings) carried from the batteries?

Figure 5.3b Mt Morgan 1906

Figure 5.4a Mt Morgan today. The abandoned open-cut mine has now filled with water (Queensland Energy and Minerals Centre)

c   Is it likely that the environment in areas beyond the mine boundary would also suffer damage because of mining activities? Give a reason for your answer.

d   What other features of environmental degradation probably resulted from the mining operations?

e   Can you suggest some reasons why mining activities like those shown were acceptable in the early 1900s?

f   Is there any evidence of the natural environment shown in the photograph, Figure 5.3b?

8   Look at the photograph of Mt Morgan, Figure 5.3b.

a   What type of mining method is being used?

b   Do you think that mining activities would be more labour intensive than today? Give reasons. Can you identify some of the work being done?

9   Compare the two photographs, Figures 5.3b and 5.4a.

a   One hundred years of mining has left a big hole! What can be done with the open cut now that mining activities

have ceased. How can the area be rehabilitated?

b   Compare both photographs in Figure 5.3 with those in 5.4. Is there any evidence of the early mine works in Figure 5.4?

c   What examples of land degradation appear in both figures? Do you think that the land in old mining sites such as Mt Morgan can be restored?

Mt Isa is an important gold producing area but 95 per cent of Queensland's copper and 40 per cent of Australia's zinc and lead is also mined there.

10 How important are these minerals in terms of value? Where is Mt Isa? What do you think would have been some of the problems associated with mining in the Mt Isa region when it began production in 1931? Consider environmental, economic and social problems.

11 Look at the photograph, Figure 5.5. Compare the photograph of Mt Isa with that of Mt Morgan 1906.

a   What are the noticeable differences? Which would you prefer to work for?

b   Where are other deposits of copper, lead or zinc mined in Queensland?

The ore from Mt Isa is shipped by rail to Townsville where it is processed to reduce bulk and add value. What is not used in the Australian market is exported as copper, silver/lead bullion and zinc concentrate.

## Bauxite, alumina and aluminium

Bauxite occurs from the decay and weathering of aluminium bearing rocks under tropical conditions. The bauxite ore is refined to produce alumina. Further refining of the alumina produces aluminium. The bauxite reserves in north Queensland are estimated at

Figure 5.4b Mt Morgan—the abandoned mine works (Queensland Energy and Minerals Centre)

Figure 5.5 Drilling into silver/lead/zinc deposits deep underground (Queensland Department of Resource Industries)

approximately 3000 million tonnes. If 10 million tones are mined each year how long will the deposits last? The Weipa deposit is the largest known bauxite deposit in the world.

Almost 70 per cent of the bauxite mined at Weipa is shipped to Gladstone for refining at one of the largest alumina plants in the world. Alumina is further processed to produce aluminium at the Boyne Island smelter. The sites of these processing plants are adjacent to a deep water, protected harbour which facilitates the export of alumina to overseas markets. The major markets for alumina are Europe and Japan and for aluminium, USA, Canada and New Zealand.

**12** How important is bauxite to Queensland's mining economy? Comment on both production and price.

## Mineral sands

The main perception of a beach is that of a recreational resource, yet the sand forming many of Queensland's beaches is rich in minerals. The minerals originally occurred in the granites and basalts of the

Figure 5.6 Weipa—bauxite mining

Figure 5.7 Gladstone refinery

mountains. With constant weathering, erosion and transportation by rivers, the minerals were deposited in the sea. Wave action carried and deposited the mineral sand to the various beach locations where they are found today.

Mineral sands include rutile, zircon and ilmenite which are the basis of a variety of commodities. Rutile and ilmenite are used as a pigment in paints, varnishes, plastics and rubber. Rutile is also used in the manufacture of titanium metal used in the aerospace industry. Zircon is the basis of refractory bricks and furnace linings, ceramic tiles and glazes.

During the boom mining period of the 1950s practically the whole east coast of Queensland was explored for mineral sand deposits and potential deposits were placed under mining leases. Because of continued pressure by conservationists, some sand mining operations, such as Fraser Island, were closed and leases in other locations have been relinquished and the beaches are now part of a national park or reserved area. North Stradbroke Island is now the only operational sand mining area in Queensland, although an application for a mining lease, in order to carry out large scale mining operations at Byfield, on the central Queensland coast, is now being processed.

---

13 Look at the photograph, Figure 5.8.
a How does sand mining differ from the other methods of mining shown in the photographs, Figures 5.5 and 5.6?
b Graph the statistics for mineral sands production and value. Is there any correlation between the two? Suggest reasons for any variation.

---

## Hydrocarbons

Two of the worlds most important resources come from a group of substances consisting of mainly carbon with hydrogen and oxygen. These are the hydrocarbons and they occur as coals and bitumen. They are also the major resources used in the production of electrical and mechanical energy.

---

14 Look at the flow chart, Figure 5.9. What are the major sources of Queensland's energy and their uses?

---

Over 100 years ago it was written: 'We may well call it black diamonds; every basket is power and civilisation'. [1]

---

15 Why is coal considered such an important resource? Of all the mining activities, black coal stands out as making a very significant contribution to Queensland's economy. What percentage of the mining revenue comes from coal?

---

Large quantities of plant and mineral matter were carried by rivers into the great freshwater lakes which now form Queensland's coal basins. These deposits were covered with sediments, compressed, and eventually transformed by slow chemical change over a period of millions of years into seams of coal. The process is called coalification. Queensland's coal was formed over 100 to 280 million years ago.

Coal is classified in various ways, the main varieties being peat, brown coal (lignite) and black coal (bituminous coal and anthracite). The coal resources of Queensland are of black coal. (Do you know which Australian state has the largest deposits of brown coal?)

The two major uses for coal are as a form of power (steaming coal) and for use in the iron and steel industry (coking coal). Queensland has estimated reserves of 9100 million tonnes of steaming coal and 7600 million tonnes of coking coal. At a production rate of 74 million tonnes in 1988–89 how long will the coal last?

---

16 Use Figures 5.10 and 5.11 and Tables 5.1 and 5.2.
a Where does coal rank in terms of production and value?
b Where are Queensland's coal fields located? Describe the distribution of the coal fields.

Figure 5.8 Sand mining —North Stradbroke Island. The hydraulic suction-cutter dredge is a powerful floating pump which pumps a slurry of sand and water to the concentrate barge located at the edge of the mining pond. Here the heavy mineral sands are separated from the slurry. The final 'concentrate' (95 per cent heavy mineral and 5 per cent quartz) is then loaded onto trucks for transporting to processing plants where the various minerals are separated (Queensland Department of Resource Industries)

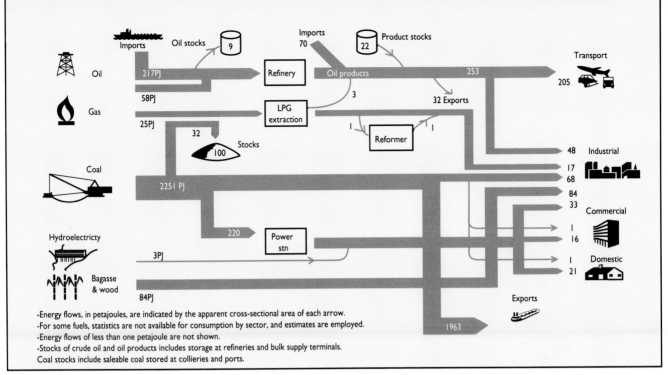

Figure 5.9 Major energy flows Queensland 1988–89

Within the diagram:

- Imports (ship icon)
- Oil stocks — 9
- Imports — 70
- Product stocks — 22
- Transport
- Oil — 217PJ
- Refinery
- Oil products — 253
- 205
- Gas — 58PJ
- LPG extraction
- 3
- 32 Exports
- 25PJ
- 32
- Stocks — 100
- Reformer — 1 / 1
- 48 Industrial
- Coal — 2251 PJ
- 17
- 68
- 84
- 33 Commercial
- 220 — Power stn
- 1
- 16
- Hydroelectricity — 3PJ
- 1 Domestic
- 21
- Bagasse & wood — 84PJ
- Exports — 1963

-Energy flows, in petajoules, are indicated by the apparent cross-sectional area of each arrow.
-For some fuels, statistics are not available for consumption by sector, and estimates are employed.
-Energy flows of less than one petajoule are not shown.
-Stocks of crude oil and oil products includes storage at refineries and bulk supply terminals.
Coal stocks include saleable coal stored at collieries and ports.

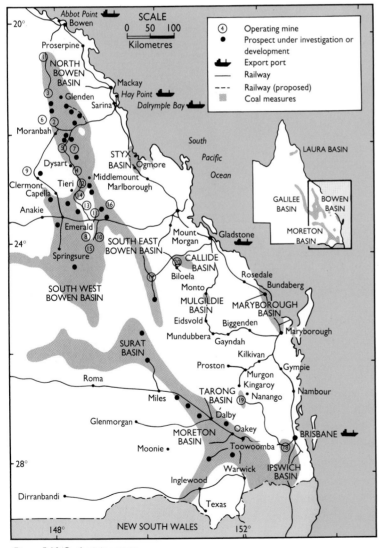

Figure 5.10 Coal mining areas

Map labels include:

SCALE 0 50 100 Kilometres

Legend:
- (4) Operating mine
- • Prospect under investigation or development
- Export port
- — Railway
- - - Railway (proposed)
- Coal measures

Abbot Point, Bowen, Proserpine, NORTH BOWEN BASIN, Glenden, Mackay, Hay Point, Sarina, Dalrymple Bay, Moranbah, STYX BASIN, Ogmore, South Pacific Ocean, LAURA BASIN, Dysart, Middlemount, Marlborough, Clermont, Capella, Tieri, GALILEE BASIN, BOWEN BASIN, Anakie, MORETON BASIN, Emerald, Mount Morgan, Gladstone, Springsure, SOUTH EAST BOWEN BASIN, CALLIDE BASIN, Biloela, Rosedale, Monto, Bundaberg, SOUTH WEST BOWEN BASIN, MULGILDIE BASIN, MARYBOROUGH BASIN, Eidsvold, Maryborough, Mundubbera, Biggenden, SURAT BASIN, Gayndah, Kilkivan, Proston, Murgon, Gympie, Roma, Kingaroy, Nambour, Miles, TARONG BASIN, Nanango, Glenmorgan, Dalby, MORETON BASIN, Oakey, BRISBANE, Moonie, Toowoomba, Warwick, IPSWICH BASIN, Inglewood, Dirranbandi, Texas, NEW SOUTH WALES

20°, 24°, 28°, 148°, 152°

c  Describe the process involved in coal mining.

One of the most important uses of coal in Queensland is to provide power for the generation of electricity. About 80 per cent of the coal used in the state is burnt to produce electricity and 97 per cent of Queensland's electricity generated comes from coal burning power stations.

Coal is also a major export. In 1989–90 Queensland's total export earnings were $11 billion. Thirty per cent of this came from the export of coal. The Queensland government earned about $1 billion through taxes and charges from the coal industry.

**17** Answer these questions.
a  Over 80 per cent of all Queensland coal produced is exported. Where are the markets for coal? Which are the most important?
b  How much money came from the coal sales?
c  Where are the ports located? Which is the most important in terms of volume?

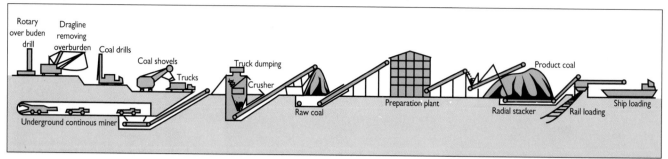

Figure 5.11 Flow chart coal mining

Figure 5.12 Surface coal mining is called open-cut or strip mining. Over 75 per cent of Queensland's coal resources are mined by this method. Surface mining is more economical than underground mining as most of the coal seam can be recovered and the accident rate of mine workers is less (Queensland Energy and Minerals Centre)

The burning of fossil fuels such as coal is said to make a significant contribution to atmospheric pollution and the greenhouse effect.

Queensland depends heavily on fossil fuels for energy resources, so are there alternatives? For example, could some of Queensland's vast uranium deposits be used for the production of electricity? The only uranium mine to operate in Queensland was the Mary Kathleen mine. It closed in 1982 when economic ore deposits were depleted. Both the mine and Mary Kathleen township are in 'mothballs' but can be re-opened if required as a source of rare earth minerals which are to be found in the tailings. The state government has ruled out the use of uranium for nuclear powered electricity generation for economic and environmental reasons so it is unlikely that the vast reserves will be used for that purpose, at least in the foreseeable future.

Why not use renewable energy resources that have less adverse environmental effects than the fossil fuels? Renewable resources contribute only a small part in energy production in Queensland. Some of the arguments against their use are that they are in their early stages of development and that costs are high compared to more conventional energy. For example only about 7 per cent of

| Table 5.3 Export sales | |
|---|---|
| **Overseas exports** | **Jan. 1991 to** |
| **By port** | **Nov. 1991 Tonnes** |
| Abbot Point | 4 728 420 |
| Brisbane | 2 967 724 |
| Dalrymple Bay | 15 833 189 |
| Gladstone | 17 274 520 |
| Hay Point | 19 625 104 |
| **Total** | **60 428 957** |
| **By country** | |
| Algeria | 334 233 |
| Argentina | 216 515 |
| Belgium* | 904 574 |
| Brazil | 1 681 990 |
| Bulgaria | 39 594 |
| Chile | 356 428 |
| China | 199 734 |
| Denmark | 1 289 575 |
| Egypt | 367 988 |
| Fiji | 21 295 |
| France | 1 786 588 |
| Germany | 268 545 |
| Greece | 110 646 |
| Hong Kong | 1 980 741 |
| India | 4 407 463 |
| Iran | 449 257 |
| Israel | 146 978 |
| Italy | 1 202 061 |
| Japan | 28 628 919 |
| Korea | 4 166 726 |
| Malaysia | 127 226 |
| Netherlands* | 2 961 101 |
| New Caledonia | 39 932 |
| Pakistan | 483 999 |
| Philippines | - |
| Romania | 592 720 |
| South Africa | 63 526 |
| Spain | 826 888 |
| Sweden | 516 685 |
| Taiwan | 2 340 121 |
| Turkey | 1 404 618 |
| United Kingdom | 2 448 436 |
| USA | 63 855 |
| Yugoslavia | - |
| **Total** | **60 428 957** |
| **Thermal coal** | **20 018 583** |
| **Coking coal** | **40 410 374** |
| * Point of distribution | |
| Source: The Queensland Coal Board | |

Queensland's households use solar power for domestic water heating because of its high capital and installation cost compared with other forms of heating. Perhaps it should carry a government subsidy so that it is more widely used.

Renewable energy is used at Birdsville where a geothermal power station produces 120 kilowatts of electricity. There is also a hybrid solar photo-voltaic/diesel system which provides 40 per cent of the electrical power for the 130 residents of Coconut Island in the Torres Strait. These two are only small projects.

Will Queensland's renewable energy resources be used more widely in the future? Should renewable energy resources be developed and used at any cost?

*Queensland has the potential to diversify its energy base through further development of renewable energy technologies, including hydro-electricity and solar power, and through the commercial exploitation of the State's large reserves of oil shale and methane gas in coal seams. These industries are to a large extent still in their early stages and it would be surprising if they have a major market impact in the short to medium term.* [2]

Should Queensland make greater use of its water resources for developing hydro-electric power? In 1982 the Queensland Electricity Commission concluded that the Tully–Millstream hydro-electricity scheme, to be located in the upper reaches of the Herbert and Tully River basins near Ravenshoe, was the preferred development for future power production. In 1987 the federal government announced that World Heritage listing would be sought for the wet tropics area and the proposed scheme lay partly

within the area nominated. This led to strong objections to the scheme by many people and by many organisations. Concerns were raised about Aboriginal heritage sites, inundation of wet tropical forest areas and the threat to endangered species, the impact on tourism with the loss of white-water rafting on the Tully River as well as other issues. In 1990 the Queensland government decided to review the project and set up a task force to investigate the feasibility of the scheme. The task force made recommendations in support of the scheme in 1991 but a final decision whether to proceed has yet to be made. Questions still to be answered include: What will happen? Will the scheme go ahead? Will there be conflict over environmental and other issues?

*The coal, oil, electricity and gas industries will continue to have a dominant influence on the Queensland and indeed the world energy situation in the foreseeable future. It is therefore essential that the State Government pursue policies which are conducive to the development of those industries in an environmentally and economically responsible manner.* [3]

The other substances which come under the hydrocarbon heading are the bitumens.

The most important resource in this group is petroleum, formed from the decay of organic material and usually found in folded sedimentary rock structures or basins. Natural gas also occurs under similar conditions. Natural gas in Queensland was first discovered by accident. In 1900, when drilling for water near Roma, the bore operator tapped a source of natural gas. It went to waste until

1906 when it was used to light the streets of Roma. This lasted for ten days and then the supply, and the lights, ran out. In the 1950s Brisbane was the first Australian capital city to be supplied with natural gas.

Australia's first oil field was discovered at Moonie, Queensland, in 1961 and from it the first commercial production of crude oil occurred three years later.

---

**18** Is Queensland still an important source of crude oil and natural gas?

a Where would you rank crude oil and natural gas in the list of products?

b Where are the oil and gas fields located? Use Figure 5.13.

c How is the oil and gas transported to the markets from the production areas?

d Queensland produces about 5 per cent of Australia's crude oil but uses 20 per cent of the crude oil products used in Australia. Where are the major resources of crude oil located in Australia?

e Other crude oil supplies are obtained from overseas. What are some problems related to relying on imported crude oil supplies?

f Crude oil and refined products are shipped to Queensland markets in tankers. What are some risks to the natural environment in using this form of transportation? Is there any alternative?

---

**RESEARCH TOPIC 5.1**

Why do you think that coal will continue to play an important in role in the production of energy for Queensland in the future? Are other Australian states placing a greater emphasis on renewable resource research and usage? What are they doing? Research the current situation.

## Mining and the natural environment

Can Queensland afford to leave some of its richest resources in the ground? The utilisation of mineral resources must continue if we are to meet future needs and continue to gain valuable export currency.

It is now very common to read or hear the words 'sustainable development' in relation to the utilisation of our natural resources. Do you know what it means? In 1987 the United Nations World Commissioners produced a report on the environment and development. The report was titled 'Our Common Future'. The report identified the need for an integration of environmental and economic objectives in order to ensure sustainable development of ecological systems. In the report, sustainable development is defined as 'development that meets the needs of the present without compromising the ability of future generations to meet their own needs.'[4]

How can mineral resources be best managed to achieve this with minimum impact on our natural environment? By the nature of its extractive process, mining activity completely alters the natural landscape. The photographs of Mt Morgan show how mining activities in the past led to severe degradation of the area in which mining took place. Do you think that it is also true today?

Mining companies and governments now have stricter and more enforceable guidelines for the protection of the natural environment than they had in the past. The Queensland government has embarked on a policy of self-regulation by the mining industry to encourage responsible management of the environment. This policy is aimed at encouraging the industry in meeting environmental responsibilities under the *Mineral Resources Act*, 1989–90, and any conditions applied to exploration, mineral development and mining activities.

---

**19** Impact of mining.

a Do you think that this will meet the concerns of people about the impact of mining on the natural environment? Do other states have similar mining safeguards?

b Why do you think mining companies and governments have strict guidelines for the protection of the environment? Is development without destruction possible?

---

Conflict between conservationists and the mining industry occurs as mining companies continue exploration for deposits of minerals and non-minerals and plan to develop these resources. One such issue occurred in 1988 when conservationists had a protracted battle with a mining company, Queensland Cement and Lime (QCL). The mining lease at Mt Etna, near Rockhampton, included a number of caves which were the home of two endangered bat species—the Mt Etna bent-winged bats and the ghost bat. Eventually, as a compromise

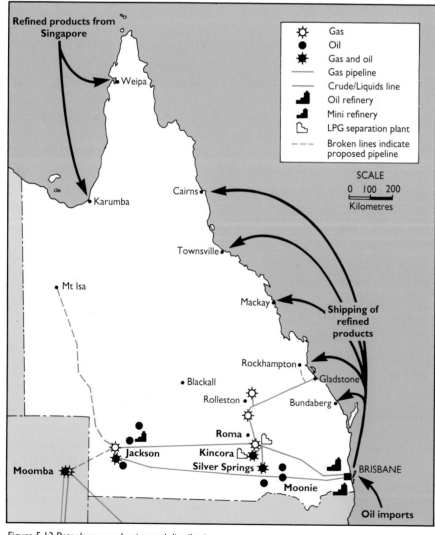

Figure 5.13 Petroleum production and distribution

## TWO SIDES OF THE ETNA ERUPTION

### CONSERVATIONISTS

The proposed extension of quarry operations will cause substantial damage to the Mount Etna cave-bearing landscape system.

There are economic alternative limestone deposits. It makes good economic sense to bring clinker processed in Gladstone from extensive Bracewell deposits of limestone to Rockhampton. The Rockhampton plant is old, much of its technology is antiquated and it should close in the interests of economical cement production and the protection of Mount Etna.

If the company is permitted to mine up the cavernous face, the quarry will be an eyesore for a great distance around.

Even caves wholly contained within the proposed reserve will inevitably be damaged by blasting outside the proposed reserve.

Elephant Hole and Speaking Tube caves, which are to be mined, are known roosting sites for the rare and valuable ghost bat.

At the time of the closest approach of the eastern quarry to Bat Cleft, unusually large numbers of juvenile bats died. At that time also, about 700 bats moved their young to a stormwater drain. This indicates the importance of Bat Cleft as apparently no other cave in the region is suitable.

### QUEENSLAND CEMENT

More than 80 per cent of Mount Etna's caves are in unconditionally protected by the establishment of a special reserve.

There are no alternative sources of limestone which are chemically and technically suitable. The company's Gladstone linker plant does not produce cement and is fully utilised supplying the South Queensland market. The company will continue to operate in Rockhampton as it has done for the past 25 years. Futhermore, a $3 m expansion is planned.

There is no way conceivable that under the existing arrangements, Mount Etna could end up being flanked on three sides by a quarry.

The company will continue to maintain a standard drill and blast extraction method on the non-cavernous face as it has done for many years. It is sheer speculation to assume that any other caves, especially within the reserve, will be damaged by quarrying of Elephant Hole and Speaking Tube.

There is no evidence to support assertions that these caves are vital roosting sites, as ghost bats range over all the 160-odd caves in the region.

The company's decision to surrender its largest mining lease on Mount Etna provides an unchallengeable guarantee of protection of Mount Etna's caves, bat populations and Bat Cleft. Every allegation made against the company has been shown to be false.

between the opposing groups, the area was declared a scientific reserve. In 1990, as a further safeguard, the caves were included as part of the Fitzroy Caves National Park.

**20** Discuss the arguments put forward by both sides as shown in Figure 5.14

**21** Reference is often made in the media to terms such as 'red tape', 'green tape' and 'black tape' which restricts mining exploration and development.
a  What do the terms mean?
b  Are they appropriate terms to use?
c  Can you give recent examples of conflict between the mining industry and each of the groups referred to by the terms?

Australia, and this can also be applied to Queensland, has been referred to as a great quarry providing raw materials for other industrialised nations.

By further processing mineral resources, employment opportunities are increased and value is added to the resource. Both the federal and Queensland state governments are now attempting to do this by supporting a number of projects (see Figure 5.15).

**22** What are these projects and where are they to be located? How will Queenslanders benefit from the projects?

## Primary resources

Primary resources are generally those that come from effective management of our soil resources and include the pastoral, agricultural and horticultural industries.

Soil is one of our most valuable natural resources. It is that part of the earth's surface that supports plant growth. It consists largely of weathered rock particles and organic matter. Soil formation includes
- the parent material from which it is derived—rock type
- landform—specially slope of the land
- time—soil forms over very long periods of time, anywhere between one or two hundred years to thousands and even millions of years
- climate—a very important part of the process, especially moisture and temperature
- the biological input of plants and animals.

---

### $3000M PROJECTS PLANNED FOR AREA

New projects valued at $3000 million are being implemented or investigated in the latest round of development in the Gladstone industrial area.

They include the first stage of a $500 million magnesium metal plant to process magnesite from Queensland Metals Corporation's vast deposits at Kunwarara, north of Rockhampton.

A pilot metal plant will be followed by a full operating plant, which will create 1000 jobs during its construction phase, 500 full-time jobs and export revenue worth hundreds of millions of dollars.

The Premier, Mr Goss, has said that the development of a magnesium light metal industry based in the Kunwarara deposits would hold enormous economic potential for Queensland.

Another industry based on the magnesite deposits, a $180 million plant producing magnesia for refractory bricks for use in steel furnaces, is already in production, just north of Rockhampton.

Other major projects under investigation include:
- An oil shale plant, estimated to cost $145 million.
- A special steel mill, estimated to cost $800 million.
- A third aluminium potline at Boyne Smelters Ltd. Cost $820 million... this project is dependent on Queensland Government selling Gladstone power station to the smelter operators, who want to control future electricity costs of smelting.
- A titanium plant estimated to cost $200 million.

The general manager of Gladstone Area Promotion and Development Ltd, Mr Peter Corones, said Gladstone could become the capital of Australia's light metal industries. It had aluminium, magnesium and titanium in the area.

He said: "The sky's the limit in the flow-on other industries."

---

Figure 5.14 (*Queensland Goverment. Mining Journal*)

Figure 5.15 (*Sunday Mail*, 15 March 1992)

Like most of Australia, Queensland's soils are old and infertile. However, there are extensive areas of moderately fertile clays and some limited areas of fertile soils such as alluvium, black earths and the red tableland soils.

**23** Answer these questions.

a  Is soil a renewable or non-renewable resource? Think very carefully before answering this question. We use soil over and over again but will it be there for future generations to use? The rate of soil formation is very slow and because of this soil is said to be a finite resource. What do you think?

b  Modern science and technology enable crops to be grown without soil and this is being done commercially, on a small scale. What is this type of farming called? Do you think that this may be the way to produce food in the future? See if there are any products grown in this way, in the produce section of your supermarket or local greengrocer's shop.

In September 1991 south-east Queensland was shrouded in dust for about twelve hours. The dust, which extended from the Gold Coast to Maryborough, was carried by south-westerly winds from central and western Australia. This was part of our land resource being carried out to sea!

Throughout Australia there is growing concern about land conservation issues. In Queensland, 83 per cent of the cultivated land is affected by soil erosion and 48 per cent of the grazing land is in poor condition.[5] In just over 100 years of farming Queensland's land resource is now suffering from the effects of various types of land degradation such as

- soil erosion by water which includes sheet erosion, rill erosion, gully erosion, and erosive flooding on flood plains
- soil salinity, caused by overclearing trees or poor irrigation management, both of which can cause a rise in salinity in ground water tables
- a decline in soil fertility caused by soil erosion and continuous cropping
- soil-structure breakdown caused by excessive cultivation and continuous cropping.

These problems are not unique to Queensland, but are widespread throughout Australia.

## Agricultural activities

The production of grains, beef and wool (as well as mining) were the original economic bases for the development of Queensland. These three primary products still make a significant contribution to Queensland's and to Australia's economic growth. (See Table 1.3.)

**24** Queensland and agriculture.

a  What share does Queensland contribute to Australia's total agricultural production?

b  What were Queensland's major agricultural commodities in 1989–90? (See Tables 5.4 and 5.5.)

c  Where are these commodities produced in Queensland?

d  What features of the natural environment determine the distribution of the major agricultural activities? Can you name at least four?

e  What can farmers do to make up for some of the deficiencies in the natural environment? Can you think of two or three ways?

f  In what ways do you think that historical, economic and political factors could influence the distribution of primary products? Can you give one or two examples of each?

## Pastoral activities

Sheep and cattle grazing is Queensland's oldest form of European type land use. As explorers first penetrated into what is now Queensland, their reports of extensive grasslands brought squatters from the south. The first

**Table 5.4 Queensland's major agricultural commodities, quantities**

|  | 1985–86 | 1986–87 | 1987–88 | 1988–89 | 1989–90 |
|---|---|---|---|---|---|
| Meat (tonnes) | 631 510 | 685 614 | 706 300 | 666 797 | 731 700 |
| Sugar cane ('000 tonnes) | 22 003 | 23 460 | 23 200 | 25 586 | 25 230 |
| Wool ('000 kg) | 65 524 | 79 913 | 78 204 | 76 294 | 88 698 |
| Wheat ('000 tonnes) | 169 | 833 | 718 | 1 550 | 1 391 |

Source: ABS, Various

**Table 5.5 Production of meat ('000 tonnes)**

|  | 1985–86 | 1986–87 | 1987–88 | 1988–89 | 1989–90 |
|---|---|---|---|---|---|
| Beef | 531.7 | 582.5 | 599.5 | 559.2 | 620.8 |
| Veal | 10.8 | 9.7 | 9.4 | 7.4 | 6.6 |
| Mutton | 10.6 | 13.6 | 13.2 | 12.5 | 16.0 |
| Lamb | 14.7 | 13.4 | 14.8 | 15.9 | 16.1 |
| Pig meats | 63.7 | 66.4 | 69.5 | 71.7 | 72.1 |
| **Total** | **631.5** | **685.6** | **706.3** | **666.7** | **731.7** |
| Queensland's share of total Australian production (%) | 28.3 | 28.9 | 28.9 | 28.4 | 31.5 |

Source: ABS, Monthly Summary of Statistics, Queensland

**RESEARCH TOPIC 5.2**

a  Choose any one of the types of soil degradation mentioned above.

b  Explain the processes that cause the deterioration of the land resource.

c  Outline some of the common methods that are being used to restore the land.

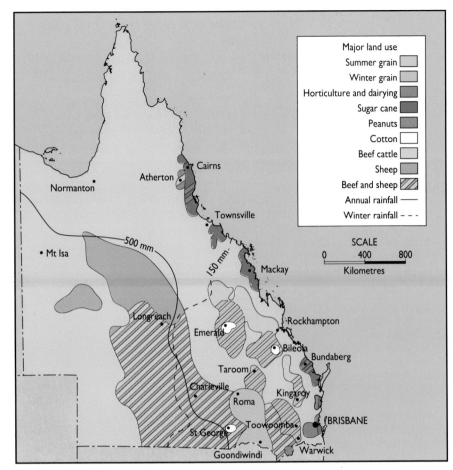

Figure 5.16 Major land use and rainfall isohyets

Figure 5.17 Droughtmaster cattle, North Queensland

such area occupied was the Darling Downs region when a flock of 4000 ewes was established near Warwick in 1840. Squatters quickly spread throughout the state forming the frontiers of settlement. The squatters were followed by free settlers who developed many of the small farms and settlement patterns that we see today. About 98 per cent of the thirteen or so million sheep in Queensland are Merino. By the end of the 1890s about five million cattle were grazing in most parts of Queensland.

The cattle population today is about double this figure. One of the biggest problems that the cattle industry faced in its development was the cattle tick, especially to the north and west of the state. The parasitic tick is a small blood sucking animal related to spiders and scorpions. The English breeds of cattle were not used to the tropical and sub-tropical conditions which favoured the cattle tick and they had little resistance to it and the tick fever it transmitted. Today 65 per cent of the beef cattle are Brahman/British cross. The animals are both heat and drought tolerant and also tick resistant. The droughtmaster is a cross between the Indian Brahman and English shorthorn. With the aid of modern science, productivity losses today are less than in the earlier periods but regular controls, preventative methods and inspections are still necessary in order to maintain the health of the livestock.

**25** Describe the distribution of the pastoral areas. Does there appear to be a relationship between the pastoral areas and rainfall? (See also Figure 2.15.)

Because of the great diversity of Queensland's natural environment there is also great variation between the grazing properties, both in size and in type of pasture. In areas of lower rainfall, cattle properties range up to 3000 square kilometres. The carrying capacity for sheep varies from 2.5 sheep per hectare in the Darling Downs to 1 sheep per 5 hectares or more in the western areas. The more intensive, fattening properties are located in the grain growing areas or in the higher rainfall regions where lush pastures permit grass fattening. Fourteen major native grasses are recognised in Queensland which are very important to the pastoral industry, especially the Mitchell grass, black spear grass and the brigalow pastures.

**26** Use Figure 5.18.
a   Outline some of the examples of soil and environment degradation in the pastoral areas of western Queensland.
b   What are some of the solutions to the various problems?
c   Is everyone in agreement?

## Field crops

The major areas of grain growing had been established by the turn of the century, especially on the Darling Downs, but have since expanded to other parts of Queensland.

## SLOW DEATH IN THE MULGA

Rural editor Gordon Collie looks at a new report on land degradation and some of its controversial recommendations.

An area of outback Queensland the size of Victoria is slipping into a degraded, useless wasteland. Kangaroos are proliferating, woody weeds are rampant and the viability of hundreds of graziers is on the line.

These are the depressing conclusions of a major report set to focus national attention on the plight of Queensland's mulga country.

The study by the Australian Conservation Foundation has painted a bleak future for a huge chunk of the outback — more than 20 million hectares stretching west from St George to Thargomindah and north almost as far as Longreach.

The region takes its name from the dominant vegetation, mulga or *acacia aneura*, used and abused by graziers since the 1860s.

The ACF chose the mulga country as one of two regions for detailed study and has just published the results in a volume entitled *Recovering Ground*.

The ACF and graziers living in the region agree that several million hectares of the fragile mulga environment are already damaged beyond repair.

There is also little disagreement about some of the fundamental causes.

They include government policy which opened the region up to closer settlement, carving up the original huge stations into blocks too small to produce a viable living; and poor management, in part forced by financial squeeze, which has led to over-grazing in a delicate ecosystem.

There are, however, divergent opinions on what should be done to halt the degradation.

One of the major criticisms of the ACF report is that it adds nothing new to the debate. The developing disaster in the mulga country has been recognised and studied for several years.

Major reports by both the Primary Industries Department and the Charleville-based Warrego Graziers Association have pointed out the urgent need for remedial action.

Important changes are taking place, slowly on the ground, and more quickly in people's attitudes.

The ACF report, with some of its controversial solutions, will at lease promote debate and might speed up some of the necessary action.

In delving into the realms of what it calls rural psychology, the ACF says Australia's cultural heritage is dominated by a pioneering mentality which sees land as an asset to be exploited and non-economic resources such as native vegetation being of little value.

It is pragmatic enough to admit changes in this mentality will be slow and hard-won.

The report quotes DPI research that about 60 percent of the dominant soil type of the mulga lands has lost most of its soil nutrients in the past 40 years.

According to the ACF, graziers must stock according to the condition of their land — ideally to use only about 20 percent of feed available at the end of summer. Average stocking rates are presently about double this level.

The report is also critical of large-scale mulga clearing in what it says is a generally mistaken attempt to create new grazing lands.

Voluntary measures should include a major extension program by the Primary Industries Department to heighten awareness.

On the regulatory front, the ACF suggests the lands Department could base rentals on actual stocking rates.

Measures to relieve grazing pressure by increasing property size are also considered.

A trend towards building larger properties has been under way for years, however, the trend needed to be accelerated.

Rehabilitation of degraded land may be feasible if native pasture cover could be regenerated by removing all stock for up to five years.

The big question is how property owners, already struggling financially, could afford to lock up a part of their land and lose all income from it.

Up to 30 percent of all mulga lands may be so eroded that it will not regenerate simply by the removal of all stock.

Expensive mechanical treatment such as furrowing and building of contour banks to retain water were likely to be economically prohibitive.

The ACF report also said it was not feasible to rehabilitate about 15 percent of mulga lands thickly covered with mature turkey bush.

Abandonment of the land was not considered a serious option.

Apart from the obvious high social costs, abandonment would simply allow the degradation cycle to continue.

The ACF considers in some detail the impact of kangaroos in western land degradation.

While conceding that kangaroo numbers need to be controlled, the report says the current management system, which relies on commercial kill quota, is inadequate and should be dismantled.

The selective shooting of larger male roos for commercial gain was not a genuine population control program.

Some rather novel notions are considered.

These include a total ban on shooting with the government paying landowners millions of dollars according to the number of roos grazing their properties.

Another would be to re-introduce the dingo in cattle-grazing areas to provide predatory control.

The report has been greeted with a deal of scepticism in grazing industry circles.

Mr Bob Martin, a retired Charleville grazier, who has been promoting western land conservation for the past 20 years, said the ACF report did not come up with anything new. "When we started out in the early 1970s, degradation was a dirty word," he said.

"Attitudes are changing. People are more aware of the damage caused by over-grazing and property amalgamations are starting to occur."

The Queensland Land Care Council chairman, Mr Wally Peart, was critical of the report and the fact that the Federal Government had granted precious conservation funds towards its cost.

He added that the ACF recommendations on kangaroo control were nonsense.

"The present management program is about right," he said. "To talk about enforcing stocking rates and property size is just ridiculous."

"How can you deny producers the right to carry more animals in good seasons when it comes down to a question of their survival?" Mr Peart said.

Figure 5.18 (The *Courier-Mail*, 23 January 1991)

**27** Use Table 5.6 and Figure 5.19 to answer these questions.
a   Which are the dominant cereal crops?
b   What other major crops are produced in Queensland?
c   Where are the growing areas?
d   Are any of these crops grown in the agricultural areas near where you live?

Queensland has a very diverse horticultural industry. Horticulture involves the growing of a wide range of crops including fruit, nuts, vegetables, flowers, ornamental plants and turf. Horticulture uses intensive and specialised farming methods with high capital investment and running costs. The

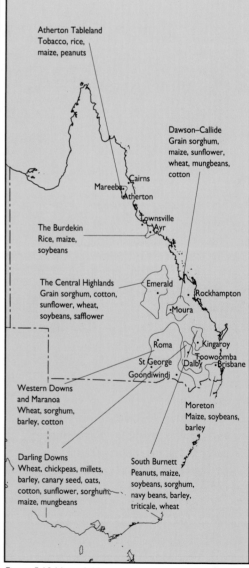

Figure 5.19 Major field crops

| Table 5.6 Queensland's major field crops | |
| Crop | % of total value of production |
| --- | --- |
| **Cereals for grain** | |
| Wheat | 47.0 |
| Grain sorghum | 27.4 |
| Barley | 16.9 |
| Maize | 6.1 |
| Millet | 0.9 |
| Rice | 0.7 |
| Oats | 0.4 |
| Triticale | 0.3 |
| Canary seed | 0.3 |
| **Total** | **100.0** |
| **Legumes, mainly for grain** | |
| Soybeans | 74.0 |
| Navy beans | 25.0 |
| Other | 1.0 |
| **Total** | **100.0** |
| **Other crops** | |
| Cotton | 35.1 |
| Tobacco | 19.3 |
| Peanuts | 19.2 |
| Potatoes | 11.4 |
| Onions | 5.2 |
| Pumpkins | 4.0 |
| Beans (mungbean and others) | 2.5 |
| Sunflowers | 2.0 |
| Chickpeas | 0.7 |
| Sweet potatoes | 0.6 |
| **Total** | **100.0** |

**Table 5.7 Main harvest months for fruit**

| Fruit | J | F | M | A | M | J | J | A | S | O | N | D |
| --- | --- | --- | --- | --- | --- | --- | --- | --- | --- | --- | --- | --- |
| Citrus | | | | | | ——— | | | | ——— | | |
| Avocado | | ——— | | | | | | | | | | ——— |
| Pawpaw | | ——— | | | | | | | | | ——— | |
| Lychee | | | ——— | | | | | | | | | |
| Custard apple | | | ——— | | ——— | | | | | | | |
| Mango | | | ——— | | ——— | | | | | | | |
| Rockmelon | | | ——— | | | | | ——— | | | | |
| Watermelon | | | ——— | | | | ——— | | | | | |
| Passionfruit | | | ——— | | | | | | | | ——— | |
| Guava | | | ——— | | ——— | | | | | | | |
| Pineapple | | ——— | | | | | | | | | ——— | |
| Banana | ——— | | | | | | | | | | | ——— |
| Macadamia nuts | ——— | | | | | | | | | | ——— | |

sub-tropical and tropical climate of Queensland is suitable for a wide range of vegetable and fruit production. On average, horticulture is the fourth most important primary industry in Queensland. Its distribution in the more fertile and wetter parts of the state is closely related to the more densely populated areas. These urban areas provide a valuable market close to the areas of production.

**28** Look at the range of tropical and sub-tropical fruits and the main harvest periods shown in Table 5.7.
a Are any of these fruits grown in or near your area?
b What advantage do you think that Queensland has for marketing these products in southern states?
c Many new exotic fruits such as babaco, rambutan, pepino, mangosteen, pummelo and five corner are now being grown. What are they? See if they are available in your local market.

## The changing nature of Queensland's primary industries

Primary industry is constantly undergoing change and evolution in response to the introduction of new crops and machinery through science and technology and the influence of world markets. One of the biggest problems faced by Queensland farmers is the fluctuating price of agricultural products on world markets and competition from overseas producers. Change and evolution also take place in farm management, processing methods and regulatory bodies associated with the industry. Farming is a business and as such it is necessary to constantly review the cost and efficiency of production. The profit made by a farmer is the gross price received for the product less all the costs incurred in getting that product to market. Capital costs include the value of the farm land as well as the cost of buildings, plant and machinery. On-going costs include labour, chemicals (pesticides, weedicides), harvesting, transport etc. With increasing efficiency in farming methods it may be necessary for a farmer to increase the farm size so that the use of equipment etc. is maximised. This purchase may involve a bank loan in order to buy more land.

**29** What other costs do you think could be included? Draw a field sketch of Figure 5.26a. On the sketch use labelled arrows to show as many inputs as you can think of. Include those visible in the photograph as well as others not seen. Use one arrow to show the output and the market.

From time to time farmers may face severe economic and social pressures. These may result from natural disasters, such as floods or droughts, inefficient farm management or an economic downturn in the farm product and/or the general economy. The economic cost is easily calculated but the social cost to a farmer and community is more difficult to measure.

**30** What do you think are some of the social costs to farmers and the general farming community in times of difficulty such as those outlined? There were many examples during the 1991–92 droughts and floods in Queensland.

# Case study: The sugar industry

Sugar provides about half the total gross value of all rural industry in tropical Queensland as well as a high percentage of employment in all of the various aspects of the sugar industry.

Since sugar cane was first grown near Brisbane in 1862 the sugar industry has undergone various changes in evolving to its current structure. The change from large plantations using indentured labour to the smaller family farms of today is one example.

**31** See Figure 4.14. Describe the distribution of the cane growing areas.

a   From the distribution, and your understanding of the natural environment of Queensland can you suggest some of the factors that are important for growing cane? Consider temperature, rainfall and other features of the coastal plains.

b   How big are Queensland cane farms? Is there a variation from region to region? What are some factors that you think could determine the size of a cane farm?

c   What is happening to the average farm size? Can you see any pattern of change between the number of growers, the price of cane and farm size? Use Figures 5.22 and 5.23.

d   What change is taking place between the number of harvesters and the area harvested? What does this suggest to you?

e   Can one farmer afford to purchase a harvester for sole use on the farm? What do you think would be the best way to fully maximise the use of a harvester?

f   Because cut cane is bulky and a perishable commodity, cane mills need to be located relatively close to the cane farms. In 1980, nineteen companies operated thirty-three sugar mills. Today twenty-two of Queensland's twenty-five sugar mills are owned by four companies. What

are some effects this rationalisation of mill ownership could have on both the cane farmer and sugar production? Consider both the positive and the negative effects.

---

Primary producers throughout Queensland are today facing many new issues and changes as governments deregulate and restructure the various primary industries and further develop the concept of sustainable agriculture. Sustainable agriculture can be defined as

…*the use of farming practices and systems which maintain or enhance*

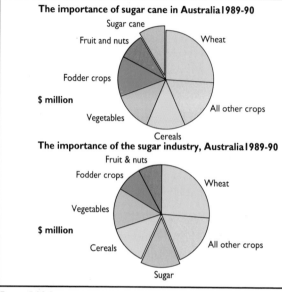

The position of sugar as a crop is shown—the graphs do not show wool or beef but simply the commodities that come from plants.

On the top we can see that cane, as a crop, lags behind wheat as a single crop, and also categories such as cereals and vegetables that comprise a number of different products, from barley and triticale to zucchinis and artichokes.

On the bottom we compare the value of raw sugar produced with the value of the other crops. It can be seen that the sugar has the second highest value of any crop in Australia.

Figure 5.20 Sugar and sugar cane are important commodities

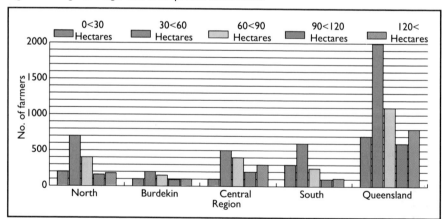

Figure 5.21 Number of farms per farm size

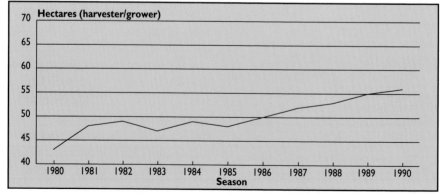

Figure 5.22 Average farm size 1980–90

- *the economic viability of agricultural production*
- *the natural resource base*
- *other ecosystems which are influenced by agricultural activities.* [6]

**Table 5.8 Ownership of cane harvesters**

|  | % of crop cut |
|---|---|
| Grower cutting own cane | 11.3 |
| Grower cutting own cane and other cane | 32.7 |
| Group of farmers cutting own cane | 11.2 |
| Group of farmers cutting own cane and other's cane | 6.3 |
| Contractors | 38.5 |
|  | 100.0 |

Source: Canegrowers

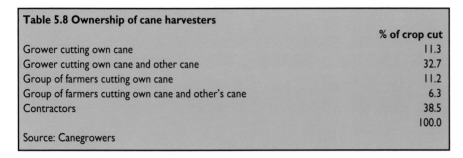

Figure 5.23 Number of growers and price per tonne grown (The figures for 1990 and 1991 have been distorted by the establishment of new farms under respective expansions)

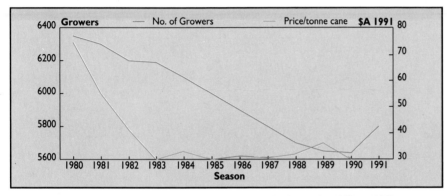

Figure 5.24 Number of harvesters and area per harvester

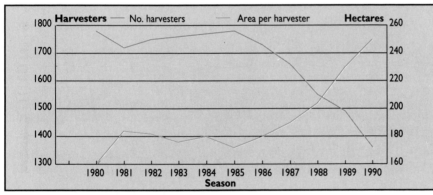

Figure 5.25 Green cane harvesting Australia-wide

The sugar industry illustrates some of these changes which many primary producers are facing as rationalisation of the primary industries is taking place.

Rationalisation is an attempt to make the industries more efficient and competitive in the market place as well as further developing the concept of sustainable agriculture.

Traditionally, cane is burnt before harvesting. Burning helps to remove leaves, weeds and other matter which can impede harvesting and milling operations. This was very important with hand cutting of cane and in using the earlier types of cane harvesting machines. The trash left on the cane field after harvesting was raked up and also burnt. Modern mechanical harvesters can cut green cane more efficiently and the need for burning cane prior to harvesting is decreasing.

**32** What has been the trend towards green cane harvesting since 1985? Green cane harvesting accounts for about 40 per cent of the harvest.

After the cane is harvested the green trash left on the field is referred to as a green cane/trash blanket. The trash blanket can provide benefits such as weed suppression, protection from soil erosion, improved soil structure and conservation of water through less evaporation and higher water infiltration. The end result leads to more efficient farming and reduced on-farm costs. (For farmers who continue with the traditional burnt cane harvest, burnt cane trash blanketing gives similar results.)

Until recently the sugar industry had been regulated by the federal and Queensland governments. The Central Sugar Cane Prices Board and the Sugar Board controlled all aspects of sugar growing and marketing. These controls included the sale and price of farms, varieties of cane to be grown, area of crop assigned to the mill, the amount of

Figure 5.26a Burnt cane harvesting. Harvesters are now a major capital cost for cane growers. In 1991 the cost of a new harvester and its haulout equipment was over $A 400 000.

Figure 5.26b Burnt cane trash blanket

raw sugar produced and its marketing. The two regulatory Boards have been replaced by the newly formed Queensland Sugar Corporation which has the responsibility of managing the Queensland sugar industry.

The federal government can protect a local industry through a series of tariffs and/or embargoes. A tariff is a tax or duty which makes the cost of importing commodities higher than the cost of the local product. An embargo is a ban on either the import or export of a commodity. In 1901 an import tariff was placed on sugar in order to protect the local industry. This was followed in 1915 by an embargo on the import of sugar. This embargo lasted until 1989 when the federal government lifted it and replaced it with an import tariff of $115 per tonne. In 1991 the tariff was reduced to $76 per tonne and it is proposed that all tariffs are removed by 1998. Not everyone agrees with the plan. The general manager of Canegrowers, the main body representing cane farmers, refers to an industry in crisis.

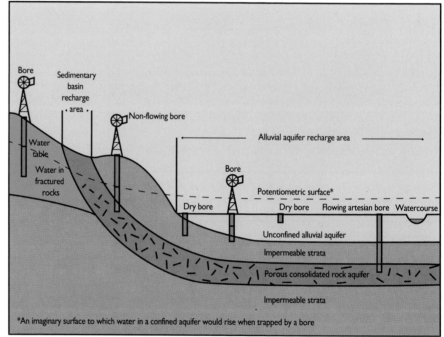

Figure 5.27 Structure of an artesian acquifer

**33** What are the major concerns of the cane farmers? What do they want?

Many other producers of primary products are feeling the effects of tariff cuts on their own products. Recently, Queensland pineapple growers have been protesting about the flood of cheap pineapples and pineapple products coming into Australia from overseas producers. The federal government claims that by cutting tariffs it will make Australian growers more efficient and cut costs to domestic consumers. Farmers claim that they cannot compete against the cheap labour, production costs and government subsidies in the overseas countries where the products are grown.

**34** Who is right? Has this issue appeared in the media recently? Discuss.

## WORKING FOR YOU

### Cane growing industry in crisis!

Dear Prime Minister...

Below is an extract of a letter sent by CANEGROWERS to all Federal and State politicians to alert them to the crisis in the cane growing industry.

WITH the annual harvest along 2100 km of Queensland/northern NSW coastline approximately 25% complete, the industry's prospects for this year are dismal. The 1991/92 sugar season is shaping up to be worse in real terms than 1985 when the world sugar price sank to a record low of US 2.5 c/lb.

We have been savaged by a combination of shocking weather (drought, then floods, then drought again) and meagre world prices (1990 average - US 12 c/lb; 1991 forecast - under US 9 c/lb).

The 1991 crop will be our worst since 1975 (the original estimate of over 27 million tonnes of cane, based on significant expansion onto new areas, has been slashed to below 21 million - 15% down on the 1990 harvest). Total sugar output will be below 3 million tonnes (1990, 3.3 m; 1989, 3.5 m).

In sugar communities an early finish to the current harvest and low farm income will mean smaller pay packets for other industry employees plus fewer jobs post-harvest.

Returns to growers this year will be below break-even point. Even the most cost-effective growers will begin to feel the bite of a cashflow drought early next year. Despite vigorous self-help programs including improved farm management methods and stringent cost-cutting, many of our growers will have great difficulty meeting loan repayments. Many will not survive a two-year period of depressed returns.

In the short term, a safety net is needed to prevent large sections of the industry from collapsing. This must include the retention of most tariffs on imported sugar i.e. the $85 a tonne tariff recommended to the IC Inquiry, and reasonable access to interest rebates under Rural Adjustment Assistance funds and social security support.

Our interests and the interests of the nation are the same. Please add sugar to your list of at-risk industries.

Ian Ballantyne
General Manager

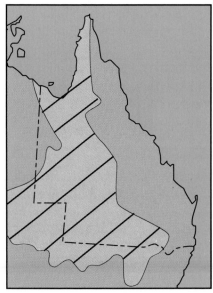

Figure 5.29 The Great Artesian Basin

## Water: A precious resource

In Chapter 2 reference has been made to the fact that Queensland's rainfall is both unevenly distributed and unreliable. This is well illustrated in the sections on flood and drought. The high average annual temperatures throughout Queensland also result in a high average annual evaporation rate, which varies from 2000 millimetres along the east coast to more than 3000 millimetres in the western parts of the state.

Queensland receives 45 per cent of all Australia's mainland water runoff, and so has good potential water resources. However, the growing urban areas and demands of an increasing population are an indication that these water resources need to be managed carefully so that future generations will have sufficient water for stock, agriculture, domestic and industrial needs. As well as surface water supplies Queensland has a good supply of groundwater. Water which percolates through the soil into the underlying strata, where it

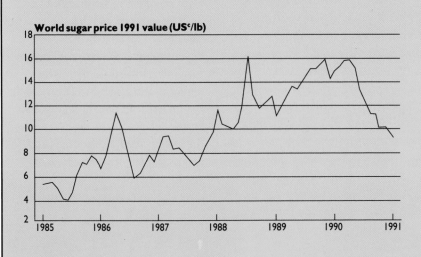

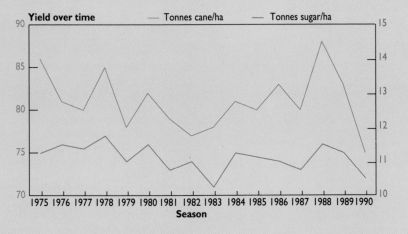

Figure 5.28 (*Australian Canegrower*, 9 September 1991)

is stored in aquifers, is called ground-water. About 50 per cent of all water used in the state is provided from this source.

One of the most vital ground-water resources is to be found in the vast sedimentary basin which underlies the extensive plains of western Queensland. Called the Great Artesian Basin, it is the world's largest and deepest artesian basin covering an area of 1 761 200 square kilometres (64 per cent of the total area of Queensland). (See Figures 5.27 and 5.29.) When comparing the location of the Great Artesian Basin with the pastoral areas and rainfall distribution it is not hard to see how vital this artesian water resource is to the pastoral industry of western Queensland. Groundwater stored in alluvial deposits along the coastal plain is also an important resource for urban/industrial, irrigation and other rural uses.

## Forest resources

Of the twelve million hectares of Queensland forests, 3.4 million is on state forests and timber reserves, of which 1.6 million hectares is available for sustainable wood production. (See map, Figure 2.6.) This represents 13 per cent of Queensland's total remaining forested area.

There are two sources of commercial timber—the native forests and the plantation (native hoop pine and exotic pines). Most of the plantations are located on the coastal plains of south-east Queensland.

Timber was one of the first resources utilised by the early settlers. Timber cutters quickly moved into the forests to log the excellent timber, especially the cedar. The coastal rivers were used to transfer the logs to the mills and

so the coastal lowland forests were first to go. The loggers were quickly followed by farmers who were anxious to clear the land. This led to conflict because the loggers wanted to preserve some areas for future logging needs and claimed that the settlers were over-clearing the forests and wasting timber.

Although there have been many conflicts over the use of Queens-land's forests in recent years, concern for the preservation of forests goes back over one hundred years. Sawmillers were eager to preserve forests in order to safe-guard future timber supplies but other people wanted to preserve some of Queensland's beautiful forests forever. It is because of the efforts of individuals in earlier days that areas such as Bunya Mountains (1908), Cunninghams Gap, Witches Falls, Mt Tamborine and Lamington National Park (1915) were preserved for use today. Citizen pressure in the 1930s also resulted in the establishment of the 50 000 hectare Eungella National Park with its unique flora and fauna that evolved over a period of 30 000 years or more when it was isolated from other rainforests by wide corridors of open forests.

This desire to preserve the natural forest environment continues and conflict over the utilisation/preservation of Queensland forests is ongoing. Although parts of the wet tropical rainforests are now protected as national parks it has not been without long and bitter struggles between people with differing viewpoints on how these forest resources should be utilised. Most recent conflict occurred over the logging in the northern wet tropical forests and on Fraser Island. The conflict over logging on Fraser

Island goes back more than two decades, but the battle reached a peak in the mid-1980s. Logging was eventually phased out and the last tree was felled in November 1991.

---

**35** What are the most recent issues concerning forests in Queensland and in your own area?

---

Queensland has a diverse, resource-rich economy and much of its present prosperity stems from this. The utilisation of these natural resources has also been the basis of its present significant overseas export market and manufacturing industry. Efforts are being made to ensure continued and sustainable development of these resources into the next century but Queensland does not exist in isolation. The development of its resource base is closely linked to national development and the problems of the international marketplace. There is also a need to diversify the manufacturing base and create a better balance between processing the state's natural resources and producing the more high-tech products needed for the future development of Queensland.

**Endnotes**
1 'Black Diamonds. The Story of Coal in Queensland', Queensland Coal Board, p. 1
2 Energy Policy Directions for Queensland into the 21st Century, A Discussion Paper, Government Printer Queensland, February 1991, p.16
3 Energy Policy Directions p. 26
4 The World Commission on Environment and Development—Commission for the Future, Australian edn, OUP, 1990, p. 8
5 Development and the Conservation of Agricultural Land Planning Bulletin, No. 1/91, Department of Housing and Local Government/Queensland Department of Primary Industries, p. 1
6 Standing Committee on Agriculture, Sustainable Agriculture, SCA Technical Report Series, No.36, CSIRO, Australia, 1991, p. 22

# Chapter 6

# TOURISM AND LEISURE

Figure 6.1 Tourists! What are they watching?

Figure 6.2 (The *Courier-Mail*, 25 January 1992)

Who are the people in the photograph, Figure 6.1? They are tourists! How important are they to Queensland's economy? Tourism is Queensland's fastest growing industry bringing more than $6 billion a year to the state. It provides for one-fifth of the workforce and by the end of the century is predicted to outstrip revenue from both mining and primary activities and provide an extra 300 000 jobs. It is also predicted that tourist spending could be as high as $13 billion a year.

One of the fastest growing contributions to Queensland's GSP is gained from net exports of tourism. In what way is tourism an export/import? Tourism 'exports' refers to interstate/overseas residents holidaying in Queensland. Tourism 'imports' refers to Queensland residents holidaying interstate/overseas. The tourist 'export' is not a material product like bauxite or wool, but it is the selling of a perception or mental image of a

place. It is the perception of Queensland that people have, through publicity campaigns or in conversation with friends, that may or may not attract them to visit as tourists. A positive image can encourage tourists while a negative image will have the reverse effect. Naturally these perceptions are subjective and very much dependent on people's expectations and interests.

---

1 One promotion campaign for Queensland tourism uses the statement 'Ah Queensland! Beautiful one day—perfect the next'.

a Does this convey a favourable or an unfavourable image? Why?

b What positive mental images do you think many people may have of Queensland as a place to visit? Good beaches and climate are two, can you name some others?

c Can you think of some negative images that may deter people from visiting Queensland? For example, some people see the Gold Coast as

having 'too many tourists' and as being 'over-developed'.

d What images of Queensland are being sold overseas and interstate? Have a look at some tourist brochures or media advertising for Queensland tourism and then have a class discussion on the mental images conveyed by the advertising material.

e The residents of a place can project a favourable or an unfavourable image to tourists through their attitude. Some Queensland people appear to resent tourists, both overseas and local, who contribute so much to their economy. Recent comments in the media and by people could well discourage Japanese and other tourists by making them appear unwelcome. Why do people hold such attitudes about tourists? What is your attitude to tourists?

f Tourism is a multi-billion dollar world industry, but it is somewhat uncertain as tourist resorts can quickly gain or lose popularity for many reasons. Can you name some? How can Queensland continue to gain and maintain an increasing share of the world tourist market?

## What happens to the tourist dollar?

Not all the money that a tourist spends on a holiday to Queensland remains in Queensland. Because tourism is big business, the more affluent countries like to ensure that some of the money that their citizens spend in overseas countries does not stay there. How can they do that? Some of the foreign investment in Queensland is put into five star hotels, duty free shops, tourist attractions and coach and tour operations.

---

**2** The Bureau of Tourism Research divided the revenue of a sample seven-day tour taken on a Japanese flight. Where did the money go? Look at the graph, Figure 6.3.

## Where do the tourists come from?

There are two main sources of tourists—the domestic market which includes interstate and intrastate visitors and day-trippers, and the overseas market. About 37 per cent of the Queensland domestic market is from interstate, largely New South Wales and Victoria, with the balance of 63 per cent from various intrastate sources. Over the past five years Queensland's growth from the domestic segment of the market has increased by 19 per cent compared to Australia's 9 per cent growth rate in domestic tourism. For the same period of years, tourists from overseas have shown a 118 per cent growth rate compared with Australia's 82 per cent.

---

**3** Look at Table 6.1.

a Where do overseas tourists come from?

| Table 6.1 International visitors to Australia ('000s) | | | | | | |
| --- | --- | --- | --- | --- | --- | --- |
| Country | 1989 Aust. | 1989 Qld | Qld's share % | 2000 Aust. | 2000 Qld | Qld's share % |
| North America | 300 | 136 | 45 | 1 171 | 679 | 58 |
| U K/Eire | 267 | 103 | 39 | 477 | 176 | 37 |
| Other Europe | 232 | 108 | 47 | 767 | 399 | 52 |
| N Z | 408 | 139 | 34 | 549 | 247 | 45 |
| Japan | 333 | 217 | 65 | 1 148 | 494 | 43 |
| Other Asia | 299 | 77 | 26 | 643 | 267 | 36 |
| Other | 89 | 38 | 44 | 242 | 136 | 56 |
| **Total** | **1 928** | **818** | **43** | **4997** | **2 398** | **47** |

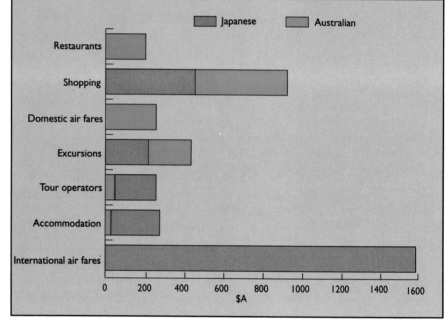

Figure 6.3 Japanese tourism spending

b What percentage of overseas visitors come from Asia? What percentage come from Europe?

c Where do you think Queensland's tourist growth market lies? (See Table 6.2.)

d What would you emphasise about Queensland to encourage people from other countries to visit? Would you use different promotional material in Asia to that used in North America? How would the material differ?

---

Although many visitors to Queensland's resort areas do so on a 'package holiday' which includes airfare, tours and accommodation, a growing number of people prefer to be 'free and independent travellers' (FIT). One such group is backpackers who prefer to spend longer periods of time in Queensland than the average tourist. They are attracted by the features of the natural environment, the safe environment for travel, the friendly nature of the residents and, in many cases, the opportunity for some casual employment.

---

**4** Look at Table 6.3.

a Who are the backpackers visiting Queensland?

b Where do the backpackers spend their money?

---

Although tourists can be found in locations all over Queensland the most popular areas are the Gold Coast, the Sunshine Coast and Cairns.

| Table 6.2 Source of overseas tourists to Queensland 1990 | |
|---|---|
| | '000s |
| US/Canada | 304.4 |
| UK/Eire | 288.3 |
| Switzerland | 29.5 |
| Sweden | 22 |
| Netherlands | 21.1 |
| Italy | 24.4 |
| Germany | 74.2 |
| France | 21.1 |
| Thailand | 19.6 |
| Taiwan | 25.3 |
| Singapore | 75.9 |
| Malaysia | 46.6 |
| Korea | 14.1 |
| Japan | 479.9 |
| Indonesia | 34.4 |
| Hong Kong | 54.5 |
| China | 23.7 |
| Papua New Guinea | 34.6 |
| Fiji | 16 |
| New Zealand | 418.4 |

| Table 6.3 Backpackers profile | |
|---|---|
| **How long they stay (average)** | |
| Scandinavians, Europeans | about 5 months |
| Americans | 18-27 weeks |
| Japanese and Asian | 27 weeks |
| **Where they stay in Qld and how long** | |
| Brisbane area | 29% one night; 4.3% more than 22 nights |
| average | 5 nights each |
| Cairns | 5.4% one night; 7.3% 9-10 nights |
| average | 13 nights each |
| **Backpacker profile in Qld** | |
| Professionals | 26.8% |
| Manager executives | 9% |
| Technical tradespeople | 15.2% |
| Unemployed/retired | 9.8% |
| Students | 11.2% |
| Solo travellers | 60% |
| Family groups | almost 10% |
| The majority of backpackers in Qld are male | |
| **What they spend (daily averages)** | |
| Japanese/Asian | $147.26 |
| Europeans | $66.19 |
| Australians/ New Zealanders | $59.53 |
| British | $55.21 |
| North Americans | $49.82 |
| Scandinavians | $47.35 |
| **What they spend in Qld (daily average)** | |
| Accommodation | $15 |
| Food | $21 |
| Pleasure shopping | $11 |
| Transport | $18 |

**5** What features of the natural environment do you think draw people to these areas?

## Growth of the built environment

Growth in the number of tourists to an area also results in an increase in the number and variety of goods and services, as well as infrastructure. In the 1960s it was the beaches and climate of the Gold Coast that attracted the first wave of tourists from the southern states. At that time a tourist infrastructure had not yet developed and services were limited, with accommodation provided by a few caravan parks and guest houses. Over the years, with the increasing numbers of visitors, a wide range of resorts, motels, high-rise apartment blocks, theme parks, restaurants, and golf courses developed. Today, many of these features of the built environment are as big an attraction to visitors as the natural environment was that led to the development of the area in the first place. Over one million people a year visit the Seaworld theme park.

Figure 6.4a Fan palms, Cape Tribulation National Park. These palms are often covered with a thick layer of dust because of the condition of the Daintree road and the heavy tourist traffic

**6** Can you name some of the features of the built environment that attract tourists to the Gold Coast?

Figure 6.4b Snorkelling on the Great Barrier Reef. How many tourists can visit the barrier reef each day without damage to the delicate ecosystem? Will a limit to numbers have to be imposed?

Figure 6.5a Gold Coast beaches and the warm climate are a great tourist asset but the area also offers a wide variety of tourist and leisure activities

Figure 6.5b Movieworld, the newest theme park on the Gold Coast opened in 1991. The tourists in Figure 6.1 were visiting this park

Figure 6.5c Sanctuary Cove, a five star resort—a residential area as well as one catering for domestic and overseas tourists

Many of Queensland's leisure and tourism activities are closely linked to features of the natural environment. With the increase in the number of tourists and the increasing demand for leisure activities by Queenslanders to these areas there is the threat of overuse, causing damage to the very ecosystem that people come to see. Already there are signs of stress and large scale degradation on some of the natural environments (see, for example, Figures 6.6 and 6.7).

Figure 6.6a Development of beach resorts has resulted in serious erosion problems along the Queensland coast. Development on or near dunes results in loss of sand from Noosa and Gold Coast beaches. Bringing back sand to the beaches is an expensive process. High rise buildings along Gold Coast beaches cast shadows across the sands

Figure 6.6b In an attempt to open up tourist areas north of Cairns in the 1980s, it was planned to cut a road through the Daintree and Cape Tribulation National Parks. This operation caused such widespread opposition that the plan was abandoned and the road left unsealed but it also left a problem that has yet to be resolved

## VISITOR FEE MAY PAVE WAY FOR DAINTREE ROAD
### By **Brian Williams** environment reporter

The Douglas Shire Council may start charging tourists $3 to visit some of the most popular rainforests in Australia.

Shire chairman Cr Mike Berwick said yesterday the council also wanted about $15 million from the State Government to upgrade the badly eroded Daintree-Cape Tribulation dirt road. He said the road was choking the World Heritage-listed rainforest with dust.

The area has become one of Australia's more exotic travel destinations and is often promoted as the spot "where the rainforest meets the sea".

Cr Berwick said a survey had shown 130,000 adult visitors crossed the Daintree River by vehicular ferry each year but visitor numbers could be higher because neither children nor locals who used the road had been counted.

He said tourists who used the district's road and facilities had contributed nothing to the area's maintenance. There were too few ratepayers in the region to support the cost of road-sealing and other improvements.

Cr Berwick said it was not known whether the council could charge the fee under the Local Government Act.

"The fee will be levied at the ferry," Cr Berwick said. "And although it won't raise all the money we need, it will go a long way towards providing facilities."

Cr Berwick said his "great hope" was that the Environment Minister, Mr Comben, would provide Government funds.

He said sealing the road would end damage to the rainforest and coral reefs.

Repairs would cause minimal rainforest damage as the existing road would not be widened.

Briefing notes prepared for Mr Comben mention council concerns about domestic animals, traffic flow waste and effluent disposal, and development plans that could lead to the rainforest's destruction.

"There is no way the area will remain a tourist attraction when the place looks like what it really is — a massive subdivision." the notes say.

District resident Ms Pauline Raistrick said it was time something was done about the road. Rains carried rainforest dirt and nutrients 5km to the ocean, where they ruined coral reefs.

"Absolutely everything is covered in dust from the traffic," Ms Raistrick said. "There's a lot more people moving into the Daintree area now and most would like to see the road sealed."

Mr Comben visited the road weeks ago and said it was a classic case of tourism gone wrong.

He said: "You get all the rainforest tours going up there … but the experience in transit is just a dust-covered, jarring ride which is ruining the tourist industry."

Mr Comben said his department would consult with the council in a attempt to find solutions to the problems.

Ms Raistrick said she could not agree with Mr Comben's statements, which included labelling the area "a shanty town".

"I don't think the place is that bad," she said.

Figure 6.7 (The *Courier-Mail*, 31 January 1992)

One of the most popular tourist attractions in Queensland is the Great Barrier Reef but the interaction of people and the reef can result in serious, perhaps long-term or irreparable, damage. Some examples of damaging human activities include

- dredging to maintain boating channels
- land-fill and land clearance to develop resorts, especially when large areas of mangroves/ wetlands are destroyed in the process
- the over-collection of species in areas without national park or similar protection
- the careless use of boat anchors and overfishing.

Tourist boats carrying as many as 300 passengers make daily trips to platforms anchored on the reef so that people can dive, snorkel and see the reef through the windows of semi-submersible vessels.

The pressure caused by the increasing number of visitors and the infrastructure needed for their access to specific areas is a growing problem. Management protection plans supported by all government authorities are necessary in order to avoid over-development and its consequences.

---

7 Use Figure 6.8.
a What plans are in preparation for the Whitsundays?
b What problems are to be resolved?

---

With the growth of what is referred to as 'ecotourism' or 'the greening of tourism' people are now wanting to visit the more remote and less accessible areas of Queensland, such as Cape York. Management programs and carefully planned infrastructure in these areas will be urgently needed if damage to the environment is to be avoided.

## Joint plan to protect Whitsundays

### By **Brian Williams** environment reporter

TOURISM pressure on the Whitsundays has prompted the State and Federal governments to prepare a management protection plan.

State Environment Minister Mr Comben yesterday released a brochure on which the public can comment before a draft plan is prepared. This would be released for further comment next year.

The plan would guide the use and management of national and marine parks in the region, near Mackay.

"The Whitsunday region is a unique continental island system supporting fringing reefs and a great variety of birds, marine mammals and turtles," Mr Comben said.

"Vegetation varies from grasslands to lowland vine thicket and the area also has significant Aboriginal and European history."

Mr Comben said the area was best known for its scenic values which attracted many tourists.

Federal Environment Minister Mrs Kelly said: "A management plan will not only protect the Whitsunday's

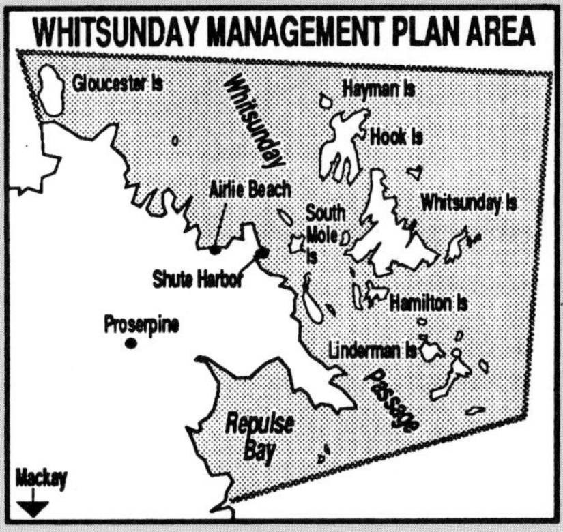

conservation values, it will also protect its tourists appeal."

Island issues which had to be addressed included fire, weed and feral animal control, provision of camp grounds and tracks and coral damage to reefs through anchors.

Conflicts between users, such as motorised water sports near anchorages and divers in popular fishing locations, had also to be resolved.

Specific areas which required management were Whitehaven Beach on Whitsunday Island, Cid Harbor on Whitsunday Island and Hook, Hardy and Bait reefs off the Whitsundays. All were suffering from the pressure of tourism.

The management plan would extend from the Lindeman and Repulse group of islands north of Mackay to Gloucester Island, south of Bowen.

Tourists spent about $272 million in the World heritage-listed Great Barrier Reef area last year.

In February this year the Great Barrier Reef Marine Park Authority said tenders would be let for thousands of public moorings along the reef to help stop anchor damage to the coral.

The management brochure is available from the reef authority and the National Parks and Wildlife Service.

Figure 6.8 (The *Courier-Mail*, 18 October 1991)

How can these areas of unique natural environments be protected? One way to protect the natural environment is through national park or World Heritage listing, but this also demands good management and management policies. With the growth in the number of national parks in Queensland and the increasing number of visitors to the most popular parks, they are being placed under considerable stress and the finance needed for their administration and protection is being spread more thinly over the increasing number.

The built environment of the tourism industry has much greater control over the impact of increased number of visitors than the natural environment. For example, the number of visitors and the price of entry to theme parks can be adjusted to meet demand. The number and variety of these parks can also be increased. This control is not so easy for the natural environment. Most of the increase in tourist and leisure activities is taking place in the Great Barrier Reef marine parks and the wet tropical rainforests. The pressure of

## Cape York councils want tourists to be levied entry fees

### By **SONIA ULLIANA** in Cairns

TOURISTS could be asked to pay an entry fee to the Cook Shire in Cape York under a plan by a local council to raise revenue for infrastructure.

The proposal to levy or tax tourists is the third of its kind to emerge from north Queensland tourist areas recently.

The Cook Shire Council chairman, Cr Robert Sullivan, said the council would consider an entry fee if the State Government could not provide $500,000 for facilities at about 17 river crossings.

Cr Sullivan said the crossings had no garbage facilities or toilets and the river beds were used as rubbish dumps by travelling campers.

He said the Cook Shire spanned 11,500ha but had only 3500 ratepayers who could not afford to pay for tourist facilities.

"The pollution made at the

river crossings at present is becoming a health hazard," Cr Sullivan said.

"There are people who want the camping experience and so they don't stay in hotels when they come to Cape York.

"They camp at river beds and wash their knickers using soap suds in our beautiful crystal clear streams. There needs to be education for tourists in an environmentally sensitive area like this."

Cr Sullivan said there were three entry points into the Cook Shire which would be difficult to supervise.

He said a gate at one main entry would stop about half of the tourists entering the shire.

The Tourism Minister, Mr Gibbs, said he could see a case for a levy when tourists had been littering one of the most pristine rainforest areas left in Australia.

Mr Gibbs said the State Government would consider the council's request for $500,000.

Mr Gibbs said areas such as Cape York, the Daintree and Kuranda were unique and there was no cause for alarm within the community that tourists would be widely taxed.

The Douglas Shire Council chairman, Cr Mike Berwick, has proposed a $1 levy on tourists crossing the Bloomfield River into the Daintree, to pay for improving roads and amenities.

Cr Berwick said the Government should assist with the cost of facilities or allow the council to charge tourists.

The Mareeba Shire Council also wants to levy tourists travelling on the Kuranda Commentary Train from Cairns to help pay for facilities such as toilets.

Figure 6.9 (The *Courier-Mail*, 11 April 1992)

increased visitor numbers is not only a threat to the natural environment but also adds to the cost of administration, maintenance and protection of these fragile environments.

Carnarvon Gorge National Park, Figure 2.1c, is one of Queensland's most popular inland parks. Tourist numbers can be more easily controlled than in other parks because of limited access roads and accommodation.

In the USA and Canada a fee is payable on entering national parks. In New Zealand many of the park services that are provided free in Australia must be paid for— including audio/visual shows, lectures by the park rangers etc. Fees are required for entry to ten New South Wales national parks as well as Uluru National Park in the Northern Territory. Perhaps fees to enter Queensland's national parks should also be paid.

**8** Tourism and parks.

a Should an entry fee be charged for Queensland's national parks? Discuss.

b How much would be a reasonable entry fee? Should the user pay? Adults pay $29 to visit Dreamworld, one of the Gold Coast's premier theme parks. Would they pay that much to spend a day in the unique environment of a national park? Would you? If not, why not? Make a list of the entry fees to a variety of leisure activities, and then discuss the issue of fees for parks.

c If entry fees are charged what specifically should the money be used for?

d Is there an alternative way to protect parks?

## Planning for predicted tourism growth

With the expected growth in tourism and the associated problems of developing resort areas, especially along the coast, planning is essential if problems of the past are to be avoided.

**9** Read the article, Figure 6.10. Do you think that management of the new Kingfisher Bay Resort on Fraser Island has the right approach?

## Tourism and leisure in Brisbane

A recent survey indicated that Brisbane does not rate very highly as a city that people want to visit. In 1992 it was ranked fifteenth as a favoured Australian destination. (The Gold Coast and the Barrier Reef gained the top ratings.)

Brisbane is Australia's largest sub-tropical capital city and a walk around the city, with its palms and other tropical plants, quickly emphasises this fact. The Brisbane River is now seen to be a great asset to Brisbane and in recent years redevelopment along its banks, the provision of parks and bicycle paths and nearby residential areas are enhancing both its appearance and its opportunities for leisure activities. The Queen Street Mall is considered one of the most successful shopping precincts in Australia, and the Brisbane Forest Park recreation area lies on Brisbane's doorstep.

How can Brisbane attract more tourists? The site of Brisbane city was fixed many years ago but by utilising its assets through careful planning and management the city can be made more attractive and offer greater opportunity for both tourist and residents' leisure activities.

## Case study: The South Bank

The South Bank of the Brisbane River was first used by Europeans as farmland for the Moreton Bay penal colony. Later it was the point of arrival for free settlers from the south, and as the river was at that time a barrier to movement further north, shipping berths and other facilities soon developed. By the 1850s it had become the centre of activity on the Brisbane River. Strong political influence of North Bank residents led to the establishment of a customs house on that side of the river which attracted shipping operations away from the South Bank.

During the period 1860 to 1880 the South Bank was no longer the focal point of shipping but had attracted a residential population of over 8000 people. With the construction of bridges, better roads and rail links, the South Bank attracted industry and commerce and shipping wharves extended along the river bank. By the end of the century it was not only a 'working class suburb' but had become a residential area for a large proportion of the 'well-to-do' of Brisbane's population who were attracted by the views from the higher land and its closeness to the city centre which had developed on the North Bank. As larger vessels came into use, shipping activity became located downstream, new bridges across the river diverted traffic from the South Bank area, commercial activity was affected and slowly the area began to decline. By the late 1970s it had lost all signs of its former prosperity and status.

The plan to use the South Bank for Expo 88 led to redevelopment of the site. A 40 hectare area of inner city urban blight, with old

### Fraser resort wants help from committee

A NEW Fraser Island resort wants to set up a consultative committee to local residents in a bid to manage the impact of increased tourist and visitor numbers to the area.

The $150 million Kingfisher Bay resort announced at the weekend that the committee would be made up of representatives of groups in the Great Sandy Region which have an interest in the development of the island.

The resort's environment management director, Mr Tony Charters, said the idea of the committee was to have a "constant line of communication" with local community groups.

"Fraser Island is an area that evokes a lot of interest from lots of different groups — from four-wheel drive enthusiasts to conservation groups," he said.

"Kingfisher Bay has got the potential, being a resort of that size, to be doing things that could upset local residents."

He said the committee was being established in recognition that the resort was likely to be within the World Heritage area of Fraser Island.

Due to be operating within the next couple of months, the committee is expected to be made up of representatives of Aboriginal, conservation, education and four-wheel driving groups plus hospitality services.

Mr Charters said he also wanted to lessen the impact that four-wheel driving is having on the island by getting the resort to sponsor training programs for visitors.

"We have sponsored a video on correct four-wheel driving techniques and we want to start some learner courses as well."

Figure 6.10 (The *Courier-Mail*, 30 March 1992)

Figure 6.11 South bank of the Brisbane River in 1960. Still evidence of some shipping activity but by the 1970s there was little left to indicate the important shipping activities that once took place along the south bank, even the two main streets running parallel to the river have now gone, These were Stanley Street, nearest to the river and Grey Street, near the railway tracks. If you have access to a street map of central Brisbane you will be able to locate the sections of these streets that remain (Surveyor-General, Queensland)

buildings, wharehouses, wharves etc. was transformed into a highly successful theme park, with emphasis on world countries. For the six months that it was open its recorded attendance was 18 560 447 people, as visitors from all over Australia and overseas came to enjoy the wide range of cultural and leisure activities. The demolition and removal of Expo 88 buildings and infrastructure left the site derelict as discussion took place about its future.

**10** Look at Figure 6.12. Can you identify: the CBD; Brisbane River; the railway line; Victoria Bridge and the direction that the camera was facing when the photo was taken? Make a field sketch to show the location of these features.

Part of the site has once again been redeveloped providing the city of Brisbane with 16 hectares of parkland, almost in the city centre, with provision for a wide range of leisure activities. A rainforest, riverside walkways and a sandy beach beside a huge lagoon are some of the features of the parkland. Three buildings, listed by the National Trust, have been left

Figure 6.12a Brisbane south bank before Expo 88. Compare this photograph with the one in Figure 6.11. What changes in land use can you see? (South Bank Corporation)

Figure 6.12b Expo 88 (South Bank Corporation)

standing as symbols of the commercial and cultural area the South Bank was towards the end of the 1800s. These buildings are the Plough Inn, one of the principal hotels of the 1880s, the Allgas Building built in 1885 as premises for a drapery business, and Collins Place, a two storey house of the same period.

Adjacent to the South Bank site and to the west are the Performing Arts Complex, Queensland Art Gallery, State Library, Queensland Museum and, on the east side, the Maritime Museum. The rest of the site will be used for commercial/retail and residential development by the private sector over coming years.

---

11 Use Figures 6.11, 6.12 and 6.13.

a Comment on the features of the south bank urban environment shown in the photograph Figure 6.11.

b The development of the site for Expo 88, Figure 6.12, resulted in some groups protesting as many people were forced to relocate as old houses were demolished and other houses were renovated increasing their value or increasing rents. Is this common in urban renewal projects? Can it be avoided? (The inner Brisbane redevelopment described in Chapter 4 highlights a changing inner city urban area.)

c What are some of the features of Expo 88? Expo 92 was in Seville, Spain. Where will Expo 96 be held? What do you think people gain from these Expos?

d Look at the photograph Figure 6.13. What leisure activities are available? What features can you see in the photograph that would be good for leisure activities? Which type of activity appeals to you? Suggest reasons why the site could enhance Brisbane as a tourist city.

Figure 6.13a South bank site after Expo infrastructure and buildings had been demolished (South Bank Corporation)

Figure 6.13b South Bank Park. This photograph was taken from the opposite direction to that of Figure 6.13a (South Bank Corporation)

## RESEARCH TOPIC 6.1

What tourism and leisure activities in Queensland would appeal to you? Plan a holiday in Queensland and incorporate your ideas. Before doing so you will need to determine what you want from the holiday. Use the following list as a guide. Write down what you would like to do or see on a holiday. Be more specific than the examples given by writing down your special interests. Many activities will be common to many places so set out the list in your own order of priority.

### Holiday leisure activities
- Relaxation—reading, watching television
- Swimming, walking/relaxing on the beach
- Water sports—boating/sailing, water skiing, surfing, sailboarding
- Adventure activities—white water rafting, rock climbing, para-gliding, scuba diving
- Bushwalking or hiking
- Horse or trail riding
- Sightseeing in cities or towns
- Sightseeing in the bush or countryside, national parks
- Visiting theme parks, such as Dreamworld, Movieworld, Seaworld
- Visiting museums, historical parks
- Visiting parks, gardens, zoos
- Visiting the theatre, opera, concerts
- Playing golf, tennis
- Dancing, going to discos
- Going to the cinema
- Eating out—in restaurants
- Shopping

Now decide where you would like to stay from the following list:
- Five star resort
- Motel
- Youth hostel/backpackers motel;
- Rented house or unit
- Caravan park
- Camping
- Stay with relatives/friends

Once you have decided on what you consider to be the most important aspects of a holiday you are now ready to decide where to spend it. Research the the various regions in Queensland and then decide which will be most suitable for your holiday. The list of the following regions may give you a starting point for your research.
- The Gold Coast
- Brisbane city
- The Sunshine Coast ( Noosa/Hervey Bay/Fraser Island)
- The Central Region (Bundaberg/Gladstone/Rockhampton)
- The Northern Region (Mackay/Townsville)
- The Far North (Cairns/Cooktown)
- The Barrier Reef Islands
- The Outback (Mt Isa/Longreach)

Once you have decided where to go, outline the various places that you would visit, what you would expect to see and the types of leisure activities that you would participate in. Can you estimate what it would cost for such a holiday?

e Can you name areas which have been redeveloped in inner suburbs of other cities, which also provide a range of tourist and leisure activities?

f Should we preserve buildings that are part of our heritage? Do they play an important role in tourism and leisure?

Some Queensland towns have built a viable tourist industry based on heritage. Longreach, the largest town in the central west is one example. The site of the first operational base for Qantas, the world's first Flying Surgeon Service and The Stockman's Hall of Fame (built as a tribute to the people who pioneered the outback) are major points of interest attracting many visitors each year.

12 Can you name some other areas that attract tourists who are interested in learning about Queensland's heritage? Do you have any heritage buildings in your local area?

South Bank Park (South Bank Corporation)

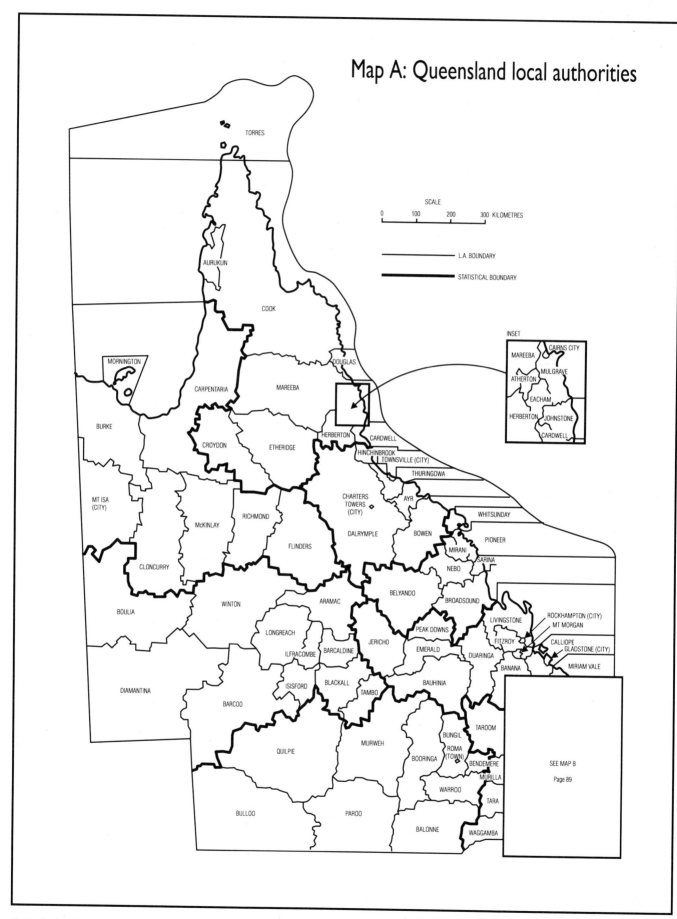

# Map A: Queensland local authorities

SCALE

0    100    200    300  KILOMETRES

———————— L.A. BOUNDARY

———————— STATISTICAL BOUNDARY

TORRES

AURUKUN

COOK

DOUGLAS

MORNINGTON

CARPENTARIA

MAREEBA

BURKE

CROYDON

ETHERIDGE

HERBERTON

CARDWELL

HINCHINBROOK

TOWNSVILLE (CITY)

THURINGOWA

MT ISA
(CITY)

McKINLAY

RICHMOND

CHARTERS
TOWERS
(CITY)

AYR

WHITSUNDAY

CLONCURRY

FLINDERS

DALRYMPLE

BOWEN

PIONEER

MIRANI

SARINA

NEBO

BOULIA

WINTON

ARAMAC

BELYANDO

BROADSOUND

LONGREACH

JERICHO

PEAK DOWNS

LIVINGSTONE

ROCKHAMPTON (CITY)

MT MORGAN

ILFRACOMBE

BARCALDINE

EMERALD

DUARINGA

FITZROY

CALLIOPE

GLADSTONE (CITY)

DIAMANTINA

ISISFORD

BLACKALL

BAUHINIA

BANANA

MIRIAM VALE

BARCOO

TAMBO

TAROOM

QUILPIE

MURWEH

BOORINGA

BUNGIL

ROMA
(TOWN)

BENDEMERE

SEE MAP B

Page 89

MURILLA

WARROO

TARA

BULLOO

PAROO

BALONNE

WAGGAMBA

## INSET

MAREEBA

CAIRNS CITY

ATHERTON

MULGRAVE

EACHAM

HERBERTON

JOHNSTONE

CARDWELL

# Map B: South-east Queensland local authorities

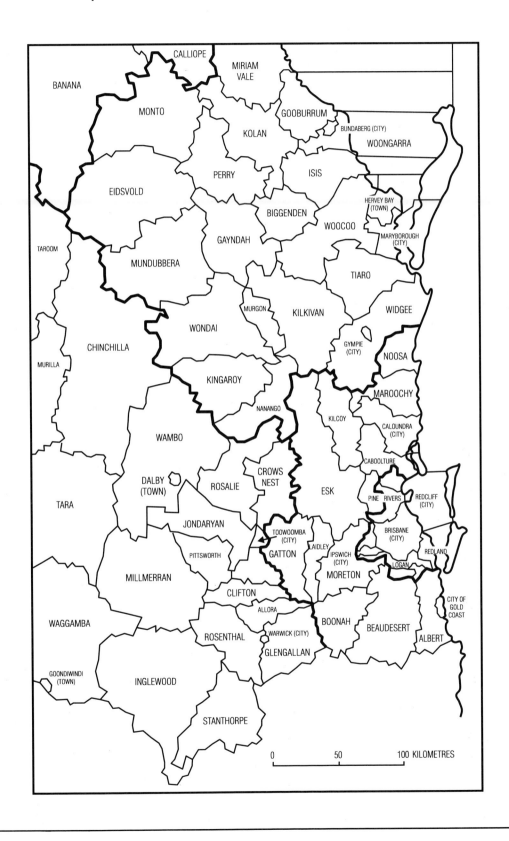

BANANA

CALLIOPE

MIRIAM VALE

MONTO

GOOBURRUM

KOLAN

BUNDABERG (CITY)

WOONGARRA

PERRY

ISIS

EIDSVOLD

BIGGENDEN

HERVEY BAY (TOWN)

TAROOM

GAYNDAH

WOOCOO

MARYBOROUGH (CITY)

MUNDUBBERA

TIARO

MURGON

KILKIVAN

WIDGEE

WONDAI

CHINCHILLA

GYMPIE (CITY)

NOOSA

MURILLA

KINGAROY

MAROOCHY

NANANGO

KILCOY

CALOUNDRA (CITY)

WAMBO

CABOOLTURE

CROWS NEST

ESK

PINE RIVERS

REDCLIFF (CITY)

TARA

DALBY (TOWN)

ROSALIE

BRISBANE (CITY)

JONDARYAN

TOOWOOMBA (CITY)

LAIDLEY

REDLAND

PITTSWORTH

GATTON

IPSWICH (CITY)

LOGAN

MORETON

MILLMERRAN

CLIFTON

CITY OF GOLD COAST

ALLORA

WAGGAMBA

BOONAH

BEAUDESERT

ROSENTHAL

WARWICK (CITY)

ALBERT

GOONDIWINDI (TOWN)

GLENGALLAN

INGLEWOOD

STANTHORPE

0     50     100 KILOMETRES

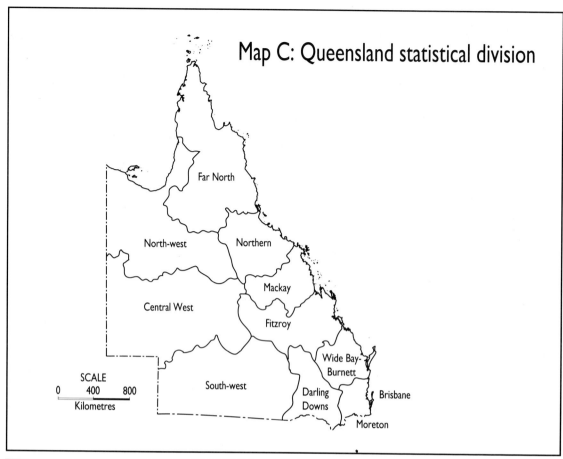

# Map C: Queensland statistical division

Far North

North-west

Northern

Mackay

Central West

Fitzroy

Wide Bay-
Burnett

SCALE

0    400    800

Kilometres

South-west

Darling
Downs

Brisbane

Moreton

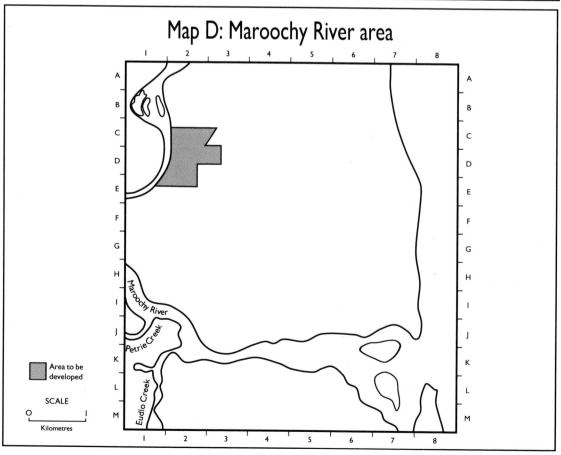

# Map D: Maroochy River area

Maroochy River

Petrie Creek

Eudlo Creek

Area to be
developed

SCALE

0    1

Kilometres

# Index